Indian Popular Cinema –
a narrative of cultural change
NEW REVISED EDITION

K. Moti Gokulsing
University of East London, London, UK

and

Wimal Dissanayake
East West Center, University of Hawaii

Trentham Books
Stoke on Trent, UK and Sterling, USA

First published in 1998 by Trentham Books Limited.

Reprinted 2003.
Reprinted and revised 2004.

Trentham Books Limited
Westview House
734 London Road
Oakhill
Stoke on Trent
Staffordshire
England ST4 5NP

British Cataloguing in Publication Data
A catalogue record for this book is available from the British Library
ISBN 1 85856 329 1

Photograph credits:
Front cover: *Lagaan*
Back cover: *Monsoon Wedding*
Reproduced by courtesy of Mr S. Chatterjee, co-author of the *The Encyclopaedia of Hindi Cinema* published in 2003 by Encyclopaedia Britannica.

Photographs on pages 30, 33, 45, 71, 73, 96, 125, 136 by courtesy of British Film Institute (BFI Stills, Posters and Designs)

Photographs on pages x and 74 by courtesy of Bombay Cine Society

Photograph on page 11 by courtesy of Rinki Roy Bhattacharya

Designed and typeset by Trentham Print Design Ltd., Chester and printed in Great Britain by The Cromwell Press Ltd., Wiltshire

This book is dedicated to the memory of beloved parents
Kumar and Jankee Gokulsing.

We thank our respective families: Sita, Shishana and Nishani Ramphul
Gokulsing and Doreen, Niru and Sudeera Dissanayake for their patience
and understanding while we were working on this book.

CONTENTS

Acknowledgements • ix

Glossary • xi

Introduction • 1

Map of India • xiv

PART I

Chapter 1
The Beginnings • 9

Chapter 2
The Distinctiveness of Indian Popular Cinema • 25

PART II

Chapter 3
Cinema and Society in India • 39

Chapter 4
Religion, Ethnicity and Caste in Indian Cinema • 55

Chapter 5
Women in Indian Cinema • 77

Chapter 6
Styles and Techniques • 95

Chapter 7
The Changing Scene in Popular Cinema • 109

Chapter 8
Regional Cinemas of India • 129

Chapter 9
Conclusion • 141

Appendix: NFDC Bombay • 147

Recommended Reading • 148

Index • 149

The first advertisement for the Cinématographe (from Garga 1996:10)

Acknowledgements

In updating this edition of the *Indian Popular Cinema: A Narrative of Cultural Change*, we gratefully acknowledge the valuable contributions of Mr Saibal Chatterjee who has authorised us to use his materials as freely as we wish; Gillian Klein for her illuminating comments, editorial rigour and professionalism and her efficient team at Trentham Books, and of Professor David Turner for his support in some of the practical processes associated with editing the new material. Our debt to all those who helped with the first edition remains. Sources and materials about Indian Cinema are fragmentary and scattered. Consequently, in putting together this overview of Indian Popular Cinema in the early 21st century, we have incurred debts of gratitude to too many people to name individually. The following, however, have helped with both their time and ideas on more than one occasion:

Cary Bazalgette and **Christine James** of the British Film Institute (BFI, London) provided us with the incentive to write this book and gave us some critical feedback in the initial stages. Staff at the BFI Library have also been very helpful.

Dr David Brottman of the University of East London helped by suggesting a framework for the book and providing critical feedback on an earlier draft of the first part of the book.

S. Vidyarthi of Books from India Ltd shared with us his encyclopaedic knowledge of Indian Cinema.

Ravi Vasudevan has made very useful comments and **Professor Sumita Chakravarty** has given advice about sources.

Rinki Roy Bhattacharya has been instrumental in carrying out interviews for us with Jagdeep and Johnny Walker, and acting as a link person for us in Bombay. She has also made comments on some aspects of the draft.

Munni Kabir, whose substantial knowledge of Indian Cinema is a boon to anyone working in this area.

Amit Bose, the former Chief Editor to Bimal Roy, has been particularly helpful in clarifying certain issues.

Iqbal Masud, the noted Indian film critic, has been generous with his feedback.

Cornel DaCosta for his steadfast support.

The Centre for South Asian Studies and, in particular, **Professor McGinnety** and **Dr. D. Gosling**, for sponsoring the book.

Wendy Childs of the Department of Education and Community Studies at the University of East London helped with the wordprocessing. **Dr and Mrs David Turner** applied their sound knowledge of computers and design to the typescript.

Although the help and support of the people mentioned above are gratefully acknowledged, they are all, according to the publishing tradition, absolved from culpability for any errors or omissions which may remain. We, the named authors, take full responsibility for the book.

from Savitri

Glossary

This glossary is highly selective, but it contains much of the basic terminology used in this book.

Advaita
A school of philosophy which says that God and Man are one, not two

Ahimsa
Non-violence

Alap
Introductory section of a raga

Atma
The individual soul in each being

Atman
Another name for the Brahman, the Universal Spirit

Avatar
Incarnation of God on earth

Backward classes
Members of Scheduled Castes and other low-ranking and disadvantaged groups (sometimes referred to as Other Backward Classes)

Bhagavad Gita
The song of the Lord, containing Lord Krishna's advice to Arjuna on the battlefield

Bhajan
Hindu devotional song

Bhakta
A devotee

Bhakti
Spiritual devotion

Bhangra
Popular music originating in the Punjab, North India

Bharata Natyam
Dance style from South India

Brahma
The Creator in the Hindu Trinity

Brahman
One of four major caste groups. Brahmans are the highest caste group

Crore
A unit of measure equal to 10 million rupees (or 100 Lakh)

Dalit
Sanskrit word meaning *split, broken* but now refers to untouchables (Harijans)

Darshan
Means to see. The act of Darshan has great significance in Hindu religion

Dharma
Has a variety of meanings – may mean religion, duty, law, morality, a divinely ordained code of proper conduct

Devadasi
A girl dedicated to temple, religious establishment or deity to serve for life

Ghazal
Form of Arabic or Persian poetry which has become a popular song form in North India

Guru Granth Sahib
Holy Book of the Sikhs

Hindutva – literally 'Hindu-ness' (Hindu cultural identity) – a political ideology of Hindu nationalism propounded by V.D. Savarkar in 1923. The key slogan used by the Hindu right wing.

Indra
A Vedic deity of clouds, rain and thunder

Jati
A kind of social group. Hindu society is comprised of several jatis

Jatra
A very popular traditional drama form of Bengal known for its 'high-pitch dialogue delivery and equally loud and melodramatic acting'

Kali
Dark-complexioned ferocious deity!

Kathak
A classical dance evolved by the traditional story tellers of North India

Kama Sutra
Unique Indian work on the art of love written by Maharshi Vatsyayana in the early centuries of Christian era

Karma
One's actions, duty. It is related to the idea of heaven and hell as well as re-birth

Karma Yoga
The path to God through devotion to duty

Krishna
Epic hero of India

Lakh
A unit of measure equal to 100,000 rupees

Lakshmi
Goddess of beauty, prosperity and wealth

Mantra
Sacred formula addressed to any deity, mystical verse, syllables recited to acquire super national powers, magical formula

Manusmriti
An ancient classical work dealing with law, ethics, morality, customs and so on

Maya
All pervading divine power of illusion which obstructs perception of reality of being

Moksha
Final liberation of the soul

Nautanki
A musical folk drama of North India

Patni
Woman as a wife

Parvati
Consort of Shiva. Also known as Durga, Khali

Puja/Pooja
Offering of flowers, leaves, fruits, music and so on to god

Purana
Ancient books which teach Hinduism to the masses in the form of stories and parables

Raga
A musical scale or a grouping of notes based on certain rules

Ramayana/Mahabharata – India's most celebrated epics. In the 1980s they were telecast on India's state television (Doordarshan) as epic soap operas and became the most popular television programme in India.

Samskara
The cycle of birth, death and rebirth

Sanyasi
One who has renounced worldly desires and attachments

Saraswati
Consort of Brahma, Goddess of Learning and Wisdom

Shiva
The great Indian god of destruction

Sitar
North Indian plucked fretted lute-type instrument

Sufi
The mystical sect of Islam

Swadeshi
Literally, of one's own country

Tabla
Pair of drums, North Indian

Tamasha
In Maharashtra, a theatre of entertainment full of dancing, singing and music

Tandava
Classical dance is made up of two constituents – forceful masculine Tandava and graceful feminine Lasya

Thumri
Type of North Indian classical vocal music

Varna
Literally, colour. One of the four large caste groups from which most jatis are believed to derive

Veda
Holy books compiled from divine revelations received by the Rishis or Sages

Vishnu
The Preserver in the Hindu Trinity

Zamindar
Landlord

Introduction

The moving image is the medium of mass culture and the most important and universal art form of the twentieth century. More than any other art form, it has the power to entertain, to educate, to reflect and to shape our sense of who we are and our understanding of the world in which we live. The moving image gives expression to our hopes and aspirations – to help us imagine what we might be.

– Imax (1996) A bigger vision, London: BFI

Really, it is a golden period for the film industry, but it is also linked to the fate of the nation, as it has been for some peculiar reason for the past 30 years... Everything looks good, burnished with gold, so Indian films automatically look wonderful. From being an embarrassment, running around trees has become a cult statement.

It is not we who have changed, it is the people who are looking at us who have. It could be at Deauville in France or at Marrakech in Morocco, or anywhere else for that matter, the world has decided to take our movies to heart.

– Amitabh Bachchan 'People first', *India Today* Special Issue January 5, 2004

In the introduction to the first edition of this book, published in 1998, we observed that until the 1980s the study of Indian popular cinema had remained largely peripheral to the mainstream of academic concerns. We quoted Mira Reym Binford's statement in a special issue of the *Quarterly Review of Film and Video*:

This special issue is devoted to the Indian Popular Cinema, a national cinema notable for its highly individual development and distinctive forms, which poses a range of interesting questions for the consideration of Western film scholars. It is little known in this country [USA] (1989:1)

Since then, a sea change has occurred in the fortunes of the Indian popular cinema, notably Bollywood – the Mumbai (Bombay) film industry. Bollywood has become part of the mainstream of world cinema with such films as *Dil Se* (With Love, 1998) and *Taal* (Rhythm, 2000) featuring in the popularity charts in the USA and the UK. *Lagaan* (Tax, 2001), for example, won the Audience Award at the 2001 Locarno Film Festival and was nominated in the Best Foreign Film category for the 2001 Academy Awards. How does one account for this transformation in such a short space of time?

One major reason is the impact on Indian popular cinema of globalisation. Globalisation is both a historical phenomenon and a way of making sense of the world. The worldwide spread of multinational capital, the transnationalisation of economies, the stupendous developments in communication technologies, the fall of the Soviet Union, among much else, contributed to its rise. The problem of understanding this new phenomenon has given rise to a new state of mind, a new style of thinking that constitutes an important consequence of globalisation. The complex and multifaceted relationship between the global and the local is most powerfully represented in cinema, and Indian cinema is no exception. It foregrounds issues of cultural modernity, ethnicity, secularism, cosmopolitanism, belonging and the diverse ways in which the nationhood is re-imagined.

Cinema emerged in India, as in most other Asian countries, as a consequence of the complex dynamics of globalism and localism. We need to situate cinema at the interface between the local and the global in order to understand its true significance. What this interplay between the local and the global has succeeded in doing, *inter alia*, is to re-focus on questions of nationhood and citizenship in terms of cinema. Thus cinema in India is crucially linked with the production of cultural citizenship. Cinema was the first institution to permit Indians to participate as citizens irrespective of caste and other differences.

Cinema in India makes available a semioticised space for the articulation of the global imaginary and its formation within the phenomenology of the local. A study of producers of entertainment films like Ramesh Sippy, Manmohan Desai or Yash Chopra makes this apparent. From the start Indian cinema has dramatically displayed the interplay of the global and the local within its discourses. Consider for example, the work of the father of Indian cinema, D.G.Phalke. Inspired by the film *The Life of Christ,* he based his film *Raja Harischandra* (1913) on a story from the Hindu tradition. Phalke was enamoured of western technology but wanted to indigenise this form of mass entertainment using cinema as a tool in the promotion of the *Swadeshi* movement – non-co-operation with the British and the boycott of British goods – which was an important aspect of the Independence movement, associated with Gandhi. Here we see the inter-animation between the global and the local.

This trend can be discerned throughout Indian cinema and reaches its climax in Bollywood films. In the 1990s, Indian commercial cinema took another turn, in keeping with the increasing cultural globalisation and commodification of society. It is perilous to talk of the evolution of a national cinema in terms of neatly demarcated decades; overlaps are inevitable. We are only using a convenient shorthand to highlight important historical moments associated with commercial cinema in India.

The 1990s saw the intensification of the interplay between the global and the local. As a consequence of the increasing exposure of Indian audiences to MTV disseminated through national and international channels, Indian film directors have found a rich new source of stylistic innovation. The pace of the films, fast cutting, superimpositions, newer ways of presenting dance sequences are a direct outcome of the influence of MTV. Films such as *Dilwale Dulhania Le Jayenge* (Lovers Win Brides, 1995); *Dil Se* (1998); *Satya* (Truth, 1998); *Kuch Kuch Hota Hai* (Sometimes Things Do Happen, 1998) are characteristic of this new trend. Except for the state-run television, Doordarshan (Distant Vision), satellite channels like Rupert Murdoch's Star Network and Subash Chandra's Zee Television (ZeeTV) appear to have profoundly influenced the sensibilities of Indian audiences. These transnational influences serve to inflect the styles, representational strategies, and regimes of signification and visual register of Indian cinema. In a rapidly globalising world characterised by the circulation and consumption of signs, this is hardly surprising.

When analysing the latest phase of Indian popular cinema, we need to examine the role of diasporic audiences, which are becoming increasingly important and influential. Diasporic audiences have existed since the 1950s but are now a decisive force on the narrative discourses, styles and techniques as well as the construction of cultural citizenship through cinema. As Mishra (2002: Chapter 8) points out, the Indian diaspora is one of the fastest growing social collectivities in the world – it is conservatively estimated at eleven million, spread virtually across the globe.

This constitutes a substantial body of potential viewers for Indian cinema. We have seen how in the past few years the responses of diasporic audiences have shaped the thinking of filmmakers. During the past decade, films like *Hum Aapke Hain Koun!* (1994); *Dilwale Dulhania Le Jayenge* (1995); *Kuch Kuch Hota Hai* (1998) have profoundly affected the imagination of diasporic

3

audiences. By their strongly articulated responses, these audiences have in turn influenced filmmakers such as Yash Chopra, whose film *Dilwale Dulhania Le Jayenge* (1995) is about diasporic experience.

This film features Baldev Singh, a newsagent who lives in London while longing for his homeland in Punjab. In his yearning to return to his cultural past, he compels his daughter Simran to marry the son of an old friend. Before he travels to India Simran undertakes a tour of Europe, where she chances to meet Raj and falls in love with him. Her autocratic father promptly returns to Punjab with his family. Meanwhile, Raj arrives in Punjab vowing to save Simran from the enforced marriage. He makes his way into the household under false pretences and renders the planned marriage unworkable. In the end, Raj and Simran are married.

Yash Chopra has made this into a highly popular film with Shahrukh Khan, the spirit of Bollywood, in the male lead. Bollywood films like *Dilwale Dulhania Le Jayenge,* in which cultural globalisation, consumerism and romantic love combine in interesting ways to create a new cultural subject display the power of globalisation. In films made in the past decade or so, we can observe a shift towards the revalorisation of the Hindu past. This is both a product of and a reaction to globalisation. Films such as *Ram Lakhan* (1989); *Kalnayak* (Anti-Hero, 1993); *Insaniyat* (Humanity, 1994); *1942 A Love Story* (1994) illustrate this trend, reflecting recent developments in Indian politics as well as feeding the nostalgia of diasporic audiences for the homeland and idealised past.

Disaporic Indian filmmakers such as Deepa Metha in Canada, Mira Nair in the USA and Gurinder Chadha in the UK have all produced films about diasporic experience which have won world acclaim. And *Bombay Dreams*, a collaborative musical by Andrew Lloyd Webber and A.R. Rahman, has been hugely successful on the London stage.

Also characteristic of films made after 1990 is the portrayal of the family as a stabilising institution. *Hum Aapke Hain Koun!* (1994), one of the most popular films ever made in India, reaffirms the value and significance of the family and arranged marriages. Romance, song and dance, which were subordinated to the depiction of brutal social violence in the 1970s and 1980s, resurfaced triumphantly here. Although marketed as family entertainment demonstrating family values, its text cleverly incorporates religious associations with *The Ramayana*, so exploiting the appeal of tradition.

There is no doubt that Indian popular films dating from the 1990s introduced into popular cinema in India a new 'structure of feeling'. This concept of Raymond Williams's, expounded in *The Long Revolution* (1961), suggests a common set of perceptions and values shared by a specific generation, and is most clearly articulated in particular and artistic forms and conventions (Payne, 1997: 518). Many elements and phenomena go into forming this structure of feeling: light, entertainment, song and dance, celebration of life, the idea of self-contentment, young love, family values, a touch of exoticism, the glamour of consumer society and the glorification of the cultural past are prominent among them.

In addition, the advent of satellite channels in the 1990s, their crossover with Indian popular cinema, the effects of new technology and the new status of the film industry itself combined to change Indian popular cinema almost beyond recognition. These developments are discussed in Chapter 7, bringing the book up to date. Also updated are Chapter 5 on women in Indian cinema and the review in Chapter 8 of the regional cinemas of India. The new concluding chapter reflects critically on the recent developments and their implications for the future of Indian popular cinema.

The main objective of this book is to provide a general introduction to Indian popular cinema — an art form that constitutes the main element of entertainment for one sixth of the world's population. We have added a list of recommended reading for students who wish to explore in greater detail some of the themes and issues raised here, particularly about the textual reading, analysis, interpretation and evolution of Indian films.

Indian cinema both reflects and is reflected through the country's political, economic, social and cultural aspects, so the book provides relevant information about India as a country. In Part I, we indicate the value of studying popular cinema and outline its historical development in India, identifying many of its key concepts as well as its distinctiveness through examples of selected films. Important themes and concerns pertinent to a critical understanding of Indian popular cinema are explored in Part Two. Consequently some films are emphasised more than others, particularly films which have achieved classical status, like *Mother India* (1957); *Awaara* (The Vagabond, 1951); *Sholay* (Flame, 1975); *Bandit Queen* (1994); *Hum Aapke Hain Koun!* (1994) and *Lagaan* (2001). But the book covers ten decades of Indian cinema and also considers a number of films which are seldom discussed but which clearly are landmarks.

Given the general lack of standardisation in transliterations of Indian languages into English, as noted by Rajadhyaksha and Willemen (1999) in their *Encyclopaedia of Indian Cinema*, we have not tried to standardise the spelling of names and films. For example, the forms Awara and Awaara, Sita and Seeta, Parsi and Parsee, Achut Kanya and Achhut Hanya, Agarwala and

5

Agarwalla, Ganguli and Ganguly are used interchangeably. Dates too are sometimes problematic – for example the *Encyclopaedia of Indian Cinema* (1999:152) states that *Keechaka Vadham* was produced in 1916 but the date was 1917 according to Garga (1996). We have provided a glossary to help clarify the Indian terms used. However, for more detailed explanations, the reader is referred to the *Encyclopaedia of Indian Cinema* (1999), to Garga's (1996) equally exhaustive study *So Many Cinemas* and to the comprehensive and illuminating *Encyclopaedia of Hindi Cinema* edited by Gulzar, Nihalani and Chatterjee published in 2003.

PART I

CHAPTER 1

The Beginnings

A Worthwhile Study

Why should we study Indian Cinema? In what ways does it help us to deepen our knowledge and broaden our understanding of the world? Are there any similarities between Indian cinema and, for example, American cinema in terms of theme, content and style that promote better intercultural exchange? These and similar questions merit our attention. In this preamble we propose to point out the value of studying Indian cinema.

India is the second most populous country in the world and the largest democracy. If present demographic trends hold, India will before long be the most populous country. Perhaps more importantly, India has a rich and diverse cultural tradition that has evolved over 5,000 years. India is pluralist and diverse in a way that few countries are. As Amartya Sen (1993: 39-40) has observed:

> It is not easy to think of another country that has as many flourishing languages and literatures. What is central to our present turmoil is, of course, religious diversity, and there again our position is fairly unique. The vast majority of Indians may be Hindus, but we have more than a hundred million Muslims (India has the third largest Muslim population in the world), we have more Sikhs than any other country, more Jains too, more Parsees as well; India has had Christians for over fifteen hundred years (much longer than Britain has had any) and while the number of Indian Buddhists today may be small, ours is the birthplace of Buddhism. I don't believe there exists another country the religious diversity of which begins to match ours.

People of Indian origins live in Pakistan, Bangladesh, Sri Lanka, Nepal, Malaysia, Singapore, Indonesia, East and South Africa, Mauritius, the Caribbean, as well as in Australia, Europe and North America. Although the vast majority of Indians settled overseas regard their countries of settlement as home, they invariably consider India as their spiritual and cultural home. However, as the *Encyclopaedia of Indian Cinema* (Rajadhyaksha and Willemen, 1994:10) noted, 'For millions of Indians overseas, a major part of India derives from its movies.' These are good reasons why we should study Indian cinema and there is perhaps no better way of studying Indian culture than through its culture-specific cinema.

India is the largest film-producing country in the world; it produces over 900 films annually. Indian films are seen not only in South Asia and South East Asia but also in East Africa, Mauritius, the Caribbean, the Middle East, Britain, Canada, Australia, the United States and the countries associated with the former Soviet Union (see Appendix). Raj Kapoor, one of the most popular actors and directors in the 1950s and 1960s, attained the status of folk-hero in certain parts of the old Soviet Union and elsewhere. Similarly, Dhondy (1985) asks:

> But what of Turkey and the reverence in which the stars of *Awaara* (1951) were held in the bazaars of the Arab world and Africa and in the remote towns and cities of the USSR? This film of the fifties broke box office records (as the phrase goes) in a hundred places, places that ancient Indian colonialism hadn't reached.

Cinema clearly opens a most useful window onto a culture and its study brings us intimacy and immediacy unavailable from most other media of communication. Culture has many definitions: to Raymond Williams, it is a 'whole way of life' and to Clifford Geertz 'the webs of significance that human beings spin around themselves'. By studying a culture we acquire deeper understanding of the customs, behaviour patterns, values, arts and crafts and the practices of everyday life of the people inhabiting that culture.

Take, for example, the caste system invariably associated with India. All societies have systems of social classification whereby people are placed in named social categories with specific attributes. In the case of India, this classificatory function is performed largely by the caste system. Although the caste system is Hindu in origin, it has influenced other religious groups in India as well. Through cinema we can enter the world of the caste system and see how it operates. As early as the 1930s, just two decades after the first Indian film was made, caste became a central issue of cinematic exploration in films like 'The Untouchable Girl' (*Achut Kanya*). A more sophisticated approach to caste can be seen in *Sujata* (of high caste), produced in 1959. Likewise, deeper insights into the complex processes of modernisation, colonialism, nationalism and freedom for women, can be acquired through Indian films. Indeed, the representation of women in Indian films is a fascinating area of study (particularly on a comparative basis with European and American cinema) and has been explored by a number of writers using mainly feminist perspectives. It illuminates dominant forms of patriarchal ideology: how women are seen as subjugated – as either the nurturing mother, the chaste wife, the vamp or the educated modern woman (Rao, 1989).

Cinema not only reflects culture, it also shapes culture. When we consider Indian films, we see how they have promoted modernisation, westernisation, urbanisation, new ways of life, a sense of pan-Indianism, secularisation, the emancipation of women and the rights of minorities and in particular the relationship between Hindus and Muslims. Even in aspects such as fashion and dress, films, aided by such film magazines and fanzines as *Cineblitz, Stardust, Filmfare, Movie*, have played a central role in Indian society and have generated discussions and influenced public opinion on issues like drugs and violence.

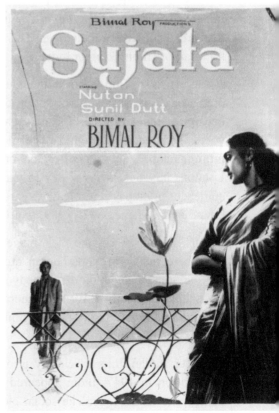

How can the study of the Indian cinema enable us to make sense of the relationship between popular cinema and Indian society? Recent advances in Film Studies have drawn our attention to the complexity of the cinematic experience. It is possible to speak of not one India but many Indias. The India portrayed in the classical Indian texts is very different from the India constructed by British travellers, missionaries and administrators and, again, from that described by novelists like E.M. Forster and Paul Scott. Then there is the India cinematised by western filmmakers like David Lean and Richard Attenborough. All these Indias are different from the one represented by filmmakers who are rooted in the soil and who grapple with the day to day lives of the people. Indian cinema allows us to study India contrastively from a different and distinct angle of vision.

By studying Indian cinema we can enter productively into the thought-worlds and performance-worlds of other traditional arts too. For example, many Indian film directors, from pioneers such as Dadasaheb Phalke to modern directors like Ritwik Ghatak and Kumar Shahani, have sought to deploy creatively the visualisations and the colour symbolisms associated with traditional forms of dance and mime, folk and classical music to enhance the communicated experience. Indian popular cinema has evolved into a distinctively Indian mode of entertainment by imaginatively amalgamating music and dance (see Thomas, 1985) and the works of such directors as Guru Dutt, Raj Kapoor and V. Shantaram bear testimony to this fact. So, through Indian cinema we can enter the larger world of Indian aesthetics.

Likewise, we will broaden our understanding of genres. There are a number of genres and styles of cinema that we constantly encounter in British and American films, such as romantic comedies, gangster films, horror films, westerns, melodramas, film noir, musicals and historical films. While some of these genres are present in Indian cinema, often as a consequence of the impact of western films, Indian filmmakers have created genres and styles that are distinctively their own. This is clearly discernible in the popular tradition of filmmaking in India.

As an art form, film is not indigenous to India in the same way as poetry, drama or dance. It is an importation from the West. However, films quickly became an indigenized art form, appealing to hundreds of thousands of film-goers. Today it is the dominant form of entertainment in India. Of its 900 million people, an average of ten million moviegoers (the population of London) buy tickets every day to watch their favourite stars. Some of the audience 'often pay a whole day's earnings to sit in the dark for nearly three hours' and, in Pendakur's (1989) words,

> are mesmerised by the slick imagery that carries them into another world where men with superhuman qualities successfully conquer all odds, including bad landlords, greedy industrialists, corrupt politicians and sadistic policemen. Women generally are the icing on the cake – upholding traditional virtues of virginity, devotion to God and family and service to men.

However, Indian films are closely associated with modernisation. At the time of partition in 1947, India appeared as the country less likely to sustain democratic institutions. The social cleavages within India, the relationship between Hindus and Muslims, the linguistic differences, were just some of the issues which threatened not only democratic institutions but the state itself. Many writers about the Indian cinema have underlined the important role that Indian films have played in building nationhood. For example, according to Mira Reym Binford (1989), the Hindi film has been seen by some as a great unifier and as a means by which the Indian self, the Indian family, the historically shaped patterns of behaviour including inherited belief systems and scale of values, are adapting to modern society. The ways that a modern Indian consciousness has emerged find ready articulation in Indian films. So anyone interested in understanding the complex phenomenon of modernisation can do no better than examine the experiences narrated in Indian cinema.

So far, our discussion has focused on the importance of Indian cinema for understanding aspects of Indian culture through Indian cinema. Indian films can afford British viewers greater understanding of the different ways in which fundamental issues of life and death are handled. By seeing films from other countries and examining them critically, we may begin to shed the parochialisms and provincialisms associated with our own limited range of experience. By seeing how others in other societies live, we examine our own culture with fresh eyes. A journey into Indian cinema and culture is a journey into ourselves.

Historical Development of Indian Cinema

Indian cinema, like most other cinemas, has evolved over time, responding to various social, cultural and political contexts and challenges. In order to understand the distinctiveness of Indian cinema, its distinguishing traits and privileged concepts, we have to examine the forces that shaped Indian films, and the changes in theme and style over the nine decades of its existence.

Only a few months after the Lumière brothers introduced the art of cinematography in Paris in 1895, cinema made its presence felt in India. The first Indian film show was held on July 7, 1896, and the *Times of India* glowingly referred to it as the 'miracle of the century'. Westerners, who were quick to realise the value of India as a site of filmmaking both because of its natural beauty and its 'exotic' culture, were inspired to make films that used Indian scenery and culture – such as *Coconut Fair* (1897), *Our Indian Empire* (1897), *A Panorama of Indian Scenes and Procession* (1898), and *Poona Races '98'* (1898).

Given the 'magic' quality normally associated with films and the potential mass appeal of cinema, it came as no surprise that Indians soon entered the domain of filmmaking. The first Indian to make a film was Harischandra S.

Bhatvadekhar, popularly known as Save Dada. He was a stills photographer, a dealer in equipment and an exhibitor of films. His interests led him naturally to the art of cinema. His first film, called *The Wrestlers*, was produced in 1899. Next was F.B. Thanawala, who made his debut in 1900. Two of his films, *Splendid New View of Bombay* (1900) and *Taboot Procession* (1900) generated great interest. The first film explored some outstanding landmarks in the city of Bombay, and the second an annual Muslim procession.

In 1901, Hiralal Sen made his mark as a film producer with a deep interest in Indian history and mythology. In 1905 film production was linked with exhibition. J.F. Madan, who had gained a wide reputation in the theatre world of Calcutta, went on to establish the Elphinstone Bioscope Company. In the years that followed, the Madan Theatre began to exercise great influence both inside India and outside. Madan was the first businessman to foresee the imminent business possibilities of filmmaking in India. Not only did he build a vast production empire on the lines of Hollywood but he also imported foreign actresses (Ermline, Patience Cooper and others) 'to act in Indian mythologicals and folk tales, as Indian females were hesitant to expose themselves to the gaze of the film camera' (Vasudev, 1995). For a time, the Elphinstone Company dominated film production in India.

By now, Indian audiences were increasingly being exposed to Western films like *Vendetta, Whirling the Worlds, The Great Train Robbery, Don Juan, Cinderella, Uncle Tom's Cabin*, and *The Sign of the Cross*. The fascination with longer narratives and the desire to see Indian experiences and characters on screen resulted in R.G. Torney's *Pundalik*, shown in 1912 and based on the legend associated with a well-known Maharashtran saint. It was hugely popular among movie-going audiences. Although *Pundalik* was the first feature film to be made by an Indian, it was shot by an Englishman and never shown as an independent film (See Rajadhyaksha and Willemen, 1994:225). The honour of making the first Indian feature film by an Indian goes to Dhundiraj Govind Phalke. His *Raja Harischandra*, released on May 3 1913, was totally Indian in terms of production, and was shown as an independent and self-contained work in its own right.

From his young days, Dhundiraj Govind Phalke was interested in poetry, drama and magic. One day he happened to see a film entitled *Life of Christ* and was inspired to make a film based on the life of Lord Krishna. As he watched *Life of Christ*, images relating to various incidents in Lord Krishna's life flowed into his mind. He came from a Brahmin household, a family of priests with strong religious roots and he brought this, along with his powerful dramatic imagination and his skill in technology, to his project.

His reverie became the 50-minute film *Raja Harischandra* which was instantly successful, due partly to the splendid special effects he created. It laid the foundation for a thriving film industry in India, and for a vastly popular genre of mythological films. One can legitimately say that the mythological film narrating the actions of gods and goddesses is a unique product of Indian cinema in the way that the Western is of Hollywood. Apart from its own characteristic heroes and villains, gods and demons, immediately recognisable costumes and settings, this genre is informed by a powerful moral imagination in which good triumphs over evil, so reinforcing the moral order. This mythological genre still maintains its mass appeal.

The successes of Phalke and Madan served to fortify the foundations of the film industry in India. Mass entertainment and moral edification were amalgamated in a way that assured mass appeal. Once film achieved firm footing as a popular mode of entertainment, filmmakers began to make their presence felt in other parts of the country. In 1917 the first feature film was made in the south: *Keechaka Vadham* was based on the *Mahabharata*. By 1920, that is seven years after the first Indian feature film was produced, Indian cinema appeared to be established on secure foundations – 18 feature films were produced in 1920, 40 films in 1921, and 80 in 1925. As cinema began to grow more and more popular among the masses and a lucrative industry was established, a number of indubitably gifted film directors made their debut; among them Suchat Singh, Dhiren Ganguli, Himansu Rai and V. Shantaram.

A good many films made during this initial period were greatly inspired by the two celebrated epics – the *Ramayana* and the *Mahabharata*. Many of the directors sought to invest their mythological narratives with a clear social message relevant to contemporary society. The filmmakers associated with this phase in the growth of Indian cinema were Janus-faced. They looked back to the past lovingly and sought to reconnect with tradition; at the same time, they sought to draw on the resources and innovations of Hollywood.

Until now all films were silent. In 1931 came the first Indian talkie: *Alam Ara*. It was a costume drama full of fantasy and with many melodious songs to intensify the audience's emotions and it was a stunning success. In that year, 27 films were made in four languages – Hindi, Bengali, Tamil and Telugu. The introduction of sound generated ever increasing emphasis on music and song. The phenomenal success of *Alam Ara* inspired many other directors to follow in its footsteps. Music and fantasy came to be seen as vital elements of the filmic experience. At times, the emphasis on music was overdone. Film historians record that, for example, the film *Indrasabha*

(1932) contained 70 songs. But what is significant is that music came to be regarded as a defining element in Indian cinema. Even to this day, some movie-goers repeatedly go to the same film because of its music.

With the spreading popularity of this new medium of mass entertainment, film directors became more audacious and explored new areas. The 1930s saw the emergence of a fascination with social themes that affected day to day living. V.Shantaram, for example, in his film *Amritmanthan* (1934), held up for scrutiny the theological absolutisms and ritualistic excesses that were gathering momentum at the time, while the landmark *Devdas* (1935) sought to explore the self-defeating nature of social conventionalism. The character of Devdas has been reincarnated many times in Indian cinema – 'the dream of surrendering life's troubles to the solace of drink in the arms of a lover/ mother is too attractive an escape to banish altogether from our secret lives' (Das Gupta, 1991:29). *Jeevana Nataka* (1942), another significant film of this period, had as its theme the baleful effects of modernisation – a love triangle in which Mohan, driven to alcoholism by his infatuation with the main actress, drives his wife to suicide.

The interplay between tradition and modernity in its various guises began to interest Indian filmmakers more and more, as evident in films like *Maya* (1936) and *Manzil* (1936). At the same time, they were toying with the diverse formulae that would readily appeal to the masses and a film such as *Manmohan* (1936) by Mehboob Khan succeeded in its broad-based appeal largely because Khan was able to fashion a formula. *Manmohan* is an early example of Mehboob Khan's 'women-centred films in which he interrogates aspects of feudal patriarchy' (Rajadhyaksha and Willemen, 1994:250). At the same time Indian filmmakers were paying great attention to stylistic and technical innovation. Their increasing exploitation of the potentiality of the medium and its imaginative reach was to be seen in movies like *Duniya Na Mane* (The Unexpected, 1937) by V. Shantaram and *Jagirdar* (Landlord, 1937) by Mehboob Khan. In *Duniya Na Mane*, for example, V. Shantaram made effective and highly imaginative use of sound, controlling it in much the same way as his visuals. Throughout the film, he used no background music, only atmospheric sounds and voices; even the few songs in the film had no musical accompaniment (Vasudev, 1995:21).

By the 1940s the art of cinematography had clearly established itself as a significant domain of mass entertainment and pleasure. Although cinema as an art form was undoubtedly an importation from the West, it had been indigenised very quickly in order to portray characteristically Indian experiences and sentiments. Even in the very early stages of Indian filmmaking, this was uppermost in the minds of filmmakers. According to D.G. Phalke, conventional accounts of the development of the Indian cinema have tended to emphasise the foreignness of the form to Indian culture – the superimposition of technology and cultural form onto a pre-modern culture. Yet contemporary commercial Indian cinema can arguably be seen as representing a continuity with Indian culture, as Phalke's writings on cinema and culture affirm. He acknowledges the Western origins of cinematic apparatus only to immerse it entirely in Indian culture.

Western influences, however, still loomed large in at least one dimension of the Indian popular cinema in the late 1930s. India's most exciting daredevil from the 1930s to the 1950s was Nadia, daughter of a British father and Greek mother. Billed as fearless Nadia, her story has recently been told by her grand nephew, Rijad Vinci Wadia (1993) in *Fearless: The Hunterwali Story*, a 75 minute film documentary. As one reviewer wrote: 'She was Zorro, Tarzan and John Wayne rolled into one. But her films had a social message too in that they frequently advocated women's emancipation'.

By the 1940s, however, a winning formula for success at the box office had been forged, consisting of song, dance, spectacle, rhetoric and fantasy. A close and significant relationship between the epic consciousness and the art of cinema had been established. Moreover, film was increasingly being recognised as a vital instrument of social criticism. It was against this background that film directors like V. Shantaram, Raj Kapoor, Mehboob Khan, Bimal Roy had chosen to make their films, films that were to generate not only national but also international interest. Raj Kapoor became a celebrity not only in India but also in other parts of South Asia, Southeast Asia, East Africa, the Middle East and the Soviet Union. Gifted film directors such as Bimal Roy, Guru Dutt and Raj Kapoor won increasing recognition for Indian popular cinema in many parts of the world. The foundations of the Indian popular cinema as both entertainment and industry were laid in the 1940s during a period of great social change and trauma for the country. Even as India was moving rapidly towards capitalism and modernisation, it was also coping with issues of nationalism, independence and ethnic and religious divisions. The popular films produced during this period offer an interesting perspective on these changes.

The 1950s

The 1950s are regarded by film historians as the Golden Age of Indian popular cinema. By now cinema was firmly established as art, entertainment and industry. However, cinema is basically an urban art the world over, and during this time urbanisation of Indian consciousness was taking place as never before. This facilitated the development of Indian cinema. Interestingly, some of the most well-known films of the time like *Awaara* (The Vagabond, 1951), *Pyaasa* (Thirst, 1957), *Kaagaz Ke Phool* (Paper Flower, 1959), *Shree 420* (Mr 420 – 420 being the Penal Code for cheats in India – 1955) dealt with city life one way or another. In *Awaara*, for example, the city was both a nightmare and a dream and in *Pyaasa* the unreality of city life is rejected.

While the popular tradition of Indian filmmaking was developing with undiminished vigour, by the mid 1950s, a distinctly 'artistic' cinema took shape, thanks to the pioneering efforts of the Bengali filmmaker Satyajit Ray. His *Pather Panchali* (Song of the Road) of 1955 won for Indian cinema great international recognition and critical acclaim. It was given the 'best human document' award at the 1956 Cannes film festival and went on to win awards at film festivals in San Francisco, Vancouver, Ontario and elsewhere. *Pather Panchali*, based on a well-known Bengali novel, realistically and sensitively chronicles the privations and hardships encountered by a Brahmin family at the beginning of the present century. If Indian popular filmmakers looked towards Hollywood musicals for inspiration, Satyajit Ray's cinematic imagination was stirred by the work of French director Renoir and the Italian neo-realists. *Pather Panchali* along with *Aparajito* (The Unvanquished, 1956) and *Apur Sansar* (The World of Apu, 1959) – generally referred to as the Apu Trilogy – are regarded as masterpieces of world cinema. After making the trilogy, Satyajit Ray went on to create such outstanding works of cinema as *Charulata* (The Lonely Wife, 1964), *Devi* (Goddess, 1960) and *Jalsaghar* (Music Room, 1958). Ray's cinema with its emphasis on realism, psychological probing, visual poetry, outdoor rather than studio shooting, and the use of non-professional actors was in sharp contrast to the practices of Indian popular cinema.

Before his death, Ray was awarded the Lifetime Award by Hollywood and was the only Indian director to be singularly honoured by President Mitterand of France, who flew to Calcutta to bestow on him the Legion of Honour. Satyajit Ray was largely responsible for the creation of an internationally recognised artistic cinema in India. Very quickly, a number of highly talented directors, including Mrinal Sen, Adoor Gopalakrishnan, G. Aravindan, Mani Kaul, Kumar Shahani, Buddhadeb Dasgupta, Gautam Ghose, Ketan Mehta, Aparna Sen, Govind Nihalani, Shyam Benegal, Vijaya Mehta, Shaji Karun emerged as able expositors of artistic cinema. Their body of work is normally referred to as New Cinema, as characterised by the qualities established by Ray. Another filmmaker and contemporary of Ray, Ritwik Ghatak, has belatedly won national and international recognition for his audacious exploration of political themes, using the strengths of artistic and popular cinema.

It is against this background that we wish to examine in more detail the forces that shaped Indian cinema and gave it its distinctiveness. Accordingly, it is helpful to the understanding of Indian cinema to analyse six forces that have had a profound impact on the growth of Indian cinema. They are:

1. The two celebrated epics – the *Ramayana* and the *Mahabharata*
2. Classical Indian theatre
3. The folk theatre
4. The Parsi theatre of the nineteenth century
5. Hollywood
6. Musical television

1. The Ramayana and the Mahabharata

From the very earliest times, the two epics, the *Ramayana* and the *Mahabharata*, have profoundly influenced the thought, imagination, outlook of the vast mass of Indian people. The two epics are at the heart of classical Indian poetry, drama, art and sculpture, nourishing the imagination of various kinds of artists, and informing the consciousness of the people. They have consequently had a profound impact on the development of Indian cinema and given it a unique Indian identity. Their influence can be usefully analysed at four levels: themes, narrative, ideology and communication. From the very beginning until modern times these epics have continued to provide Indian filmmakers with plots and themes. The very first Indian film, *Raja Harischandra* (1913), was based on the *Ramayana*, and since then scores of filmmakers have mined this and the *Mahabharata* for plots and themes. In addition, certain topics associated with motherhood, patrimony and revenge as, for example, articulated in films such as *Mother India* (1957), *Awaara* (1951) and *Zanjeer* (Chains, 1947) are directly traceable to these epics.

What is distinctive about Indian cinema can be best understood by examining its narrative structure. Despite the fact that, as we discuss later, Indian cinema was greatly influenced by Hollywood, its narrative structures with endless digressions, detours, plots within plots, remain unmistakably Indian. Here again the influence of the *Ramayana* and the *Mahabharata* is very clear. Instead of the linear and direct narratives realistically conceived found in Hollywood films, Indian popular cinema offers us a structure of narrative which can most productively be understood in terms of the art of story-telling characteristic of the two venerated epics.

Consider next the question of ideology. Despite various attempts at social analysis, highlighting the disparities between the rich and the poor, and underlining the need for social justice, it can legitimately be said that Indian popular cinema is committed to the maintenance of the *status quo*. The nature of the economics of film production and the distribution system being what they are, this is hardly surprising. For example, if we take a film director like Raj Kapoor, who was extremely popular in the 1950s and 1960s, we see how he skilfully deployed melodrama, music and spectacle to create a cinema of security that did not fundamentally challenge the *status quo*. This applies equally to most other filmmakers, past and present, in India. The central ideology underpinning the two epics is one of preserving the existing social order and its privileged values. As Mishra (1985) observes, because the *Ramayana* and the *Mahabharata* were ideological instruments employed for the expansion of values and beliefs endorsed by the ruling classes, there is also a significant way in which the Indian popular cinema legitimises its own existence through a reinscription of its values onto those of the two epics.

The important link that exists between the two epics and mainstream Indian cinema can also be usefully understood in terms of the idea of communication. The epics were transmitted orally and were closely related to ritual and folk performance. Being at the core of Indian culture, they found articulation in a variety of ways and forms in local narratives. What this promoted was the proliferation of diverse narratives and performances within the solidly established matrix of the epics. Similarly, Indian popular cinema can be understood in relation to this analogy between the two epics and their endless performances. The discourse of the Indian popular cinema, as with the epics, has its basic text, and the different movies that are made can be likened to the diverse epic performances and narratives. To discuss the linkages between the two epics and Indian popular cinema in terms of themes, narrative, ideology and communication is to open up an important dimension of the discourse of Indian cinema.

2. Classical Indian Theatre
Sanskrit theatre constitutes one of the richest and most sophisticated expressions of classical Indian culture. It was highly stylised, and its mode of presentation was episodic, laying the utmost emphasis on spectacle. In it, music and mime intermingled to create a distinct theatrical experience. It was highly conventional and specified instructions regarding the portrayal of characters. A number of features of classical Indian drama have an interesting bearing on the structure of Indian popular cinema. Sanskrit plays were highly spectacular dance-dramas as opposed to the tightly-organised realistic plays of the West. As much of the force and vigour of the classical Indian theatre was derived from conventional and traditional vocabulary of theatrical expression, the more one was acquainted with the tradition, the

better equipped one was to participate in the dramatic experience. The idea of theatre, the dramatic presentation and the make-believe of Indians were shaped to a large extent by the nature and structure of Sanskrit theatre, and it is not surprising that the classical theatre exercised a formative influence on the sensibility of Indian filmmakers. Some of the traits of classical Indian theatre that we have identified can be seen in Indian cinema as well.

3. Folk Theatre

For a number of reasons, Sanskrit drama began to decline after the tenth century. Concurrently, numerous dramatic forms sprang up or matured in different provinces which, albeit of an unrefined nature, preserved and embodied the essence of the Classical theatrical tradition. The *Yatra* of Bengal, *Ram Lila* and *Krishna Lila* of Uttar Pradesh, *Tamasha* of Maharashtra, *Nautanki* of Rajasthan, *Bhavai* of Gujarat, *Terukkuttu* of Tamilnadu, *Vithinatakam* of Andhra and *Yakshagana* of Karnataka are perhaps the most prominent among them. These regional folk-dramas, which are basically the work of untutored peasants, have one important feature in common: in varying degrees of competence and authenticity, they embody in a living form the characteristic features of the classical Indian theatre. An examination of the central features of these regional folk-dramas brings to light the fact that they have been inflected by, and carry over, the style and techniques of the classical theatre. In the use of song and dance, humour, the structure of narrative, the informing melodramatic imagination, these folk plays had far reaching impact on the sensibility of Indian popular filmmakers.

4. The Parsi Theatre

This came into existence in the nineteenth century. The Parsis were generally rich, talented and versatile, partly because of the lack of a deep-rooted cultural tradition of their own in the Indian soil, and they took up drama in both Hindustani and Gujarati. During the nineteenth century, the Parsis, who had gained a wide reputation as talented playwrights and skilful technicians, influenced the theatre of both north and south India. There were several Parsi theatrical companies touring the country and performing before huge and appreciative audiences. Some of them, like the Elphinstone Dramatic Company of Bombay, visited neighbouring countries and played before large and enthusiastic theatre-going audiences. These dramatists took a practical stance to their work and were primarily motivated by commercial success. The Parsi theatre excelled in historical and social dramas. Stylistically, the plays displayed a curious mixture of realism and fantasy, music and dialogue, narrative and spectacle and stage ingenuity, all combined within the framework of melodrama. The Parsi theatre, with its lilting songs, bawdy humour, *bons mots*, sensationalism and dazzling stagecraft were designed to appeal to the broad mass of people, and they did. Elitist critics used epithets such as 'hybrid', 'coarse', 'vulgar', 'melodramatic', 'sensational' to describe these plays. The Parsi theatre, which drew upon both Western and Indian forms of entertainment, constituted an effort to appeal to the lowest common denominator. These plays bear a strong resemblance to the generality of Indian films of the popular type. If the folk plays were based in rural areas and presented the vocabulary of traditionally inherited theatrical expression, the Parsi theatre signified an urban theatre exposed to Western modes of entertainment and production of pleasure. Indeed, one of the greatest Indian filmmakers was the Parsi Sohrab Modi, whose *Jhansi Ki Rani* (The Tiger and the Flame, 1953) was India's first technicolour film. A close analysis of the Parsi plays and Indian popular films would bring to light remarkable similarities in terms of themes, narratives, generation of emotion and styles of presentation.

5. Hollywood

Asian audiences were enthralled by the magic of Hollywood cinema. This is certainly the case in India where filmmakers very quickly succeeded in adapting the ethos, resources and inventiveness of Hollywood to suit indigenous tastes, sensibilities and outlooks. Indian filmmakers were fascinated by the technical inventiveness of their Hollywood counterparts and tried to emulate them in creating colourful worlds of fantasy. The glamour associated with the star system and the commercial advantageous-ness of the studio system were also quickly adopted. On many occasions, story lines, characters and sequences were lifted bodily from Hollywood films and reshaped to suit indigenous sensibilities. In addition, different film directors were enthralled by different aspects and artists associated with Hollywood cinema. For example, Raj Kapoor was a great admirer of the work of Charlie Chaplin, Harold Lloyd, Laurel and Hardy, Buster Keaton and the Marx brothers. It was Chaplin above all who stirred his deepest comic imagination. Raj Kapoor largely succeeded in indigenising Chaplin in a way that would attract a vast mass of film-goers.

Hollywood musicals held a great fascination for many Indian filmmakers. They related in interesting ways to the defining traits of Indian theatre and performance. The heyday of Hollywood musicals was from the 1930s to 1950s and many had a theme of the world of entertainment itself. The plots of these films were conventional. The music and spectacle enabled the characters in the story, as well as the spectators, to indulge in flights of fancy. The apparent disparity between narrative and spectacle was reconciled through the working out of the plot. This, however, is not a feature commonly seen in Indian films.

While drawing heavily on Hollywood musicals, the Indian popular cinema adopted a different strategy: the plot was not used to heal the split between narrative and spectacle. Instead, song and dance sequences were and are used as natural expressions of emotions and situations emerging from everyday life. The Hollywood musical maintained the facade of reality by legitimating the spectacle, for example *Singing in the Rain* (1952) not only deployed singing and dancing but was actually about singing and dancing. The Indian filmmakers, on the other hand, while seeking to enhance the element of fantasy through music, dance and spectacle, created the impression that songs and dances are the natural and logical mode of articulation of emotion in the given situation. Music constitutes a vital ingredient in the cultural construction of emotion. So although Indian filmmakers drew heavily upon Hollywood musicals, there are points of difference between the two forms of mass entertainment.

Commercial filmmakers in India also departed significantly from some of the conventions and norms adhered to by Hollywood filmmakers. For example, one of the central tenets of Hollywood filmmaking is to conceal the artifice, the constructedness of the effort. All aspects of movie production were regarded as subsidiary to the presentation of a realistic narrative. Consequently, camera angles were largely at eye-level; lighting was unobtrusive; framing focused on the central action of a given scene; cuts were made at logical junctures in the flow of narrative. In this way, the Hollywood filmmakers sought to foster an illusion of reality and to encourage ready identification of audiences with characters on the screen. Indian cinema, on the other hand, grew out of different roots, and there was never a strongly felt need to conform to the 'invisible style' preferred by Hollywood. So while Indian filmmakers were greatly indebted to Hollywood, they also departed in significant ways from the work produced by Hollywood film directors.

6. Musical Television (MTV)

This is a comparatively new force, making its impact felt somewhere in the 1980s. The impact of music television (MTV) disseminated through international channels is very evident in Indian popular films made in the late 1980s and 1990s.

The pace of the films, the quick cutting, dance sequences, camera angles that one associates with modern musical television find clear analogies in modern Indian films. One has only to examine the work of a filmmaker such as Mani Rathnam to recognise this. As modern Indian audiences are more and more exposed to music television programmes and these innovative techniques of presentation, their sensibilities are obviously beginning to be shaped by them. Naturally, contemporary Indian filmmakers, in order to maintain their mass appeal, are drawing significantly on the techniques of MTV. This is hardly surprising since films are where art and technology meet. It is the soundtrack which helps to construct the 'image' of a film and, although the relationship between filmmakers and technology has not always been easy, new technologies – e.g. digital images and virtual reality – are winning. The huge success of *Jurassic Park* in Hindi is recent proof.

Milestones of the Talking Films in India

First talking picture of India	*Alam Ara* (Hindi) directed by Khan Bahadur Ardeshir Irani (1931)
First Bengali Talkie	*Jamai Sasthi* directed by Amar Chaudhuri (1931)
First Tamil Talkie	*Kalidas* directed by H.M.Reddi (1931)
First Telugu Talkie	*Bhaktha Prahlada* directed by H.M. Reddi (1931)
First Marathi Talkie	*Ayodhyecha Raja* directed by V.Shantaram (1932)
First Gujrati Talkie	*Narasinha Mehta* directed by Nanubai Vakil (1932)
First Assamese Talkie	*Joymati* directed by Prasad Agarwala (1935)
First Oriya Talkie	*Sita Bibaha* (1936) directed by Mohan Goswami
First Punjabi Talkie	*Pind Di Kudi* directed by K.D.Mehra (1936)
First Malayalam Talkie	*Balam* directed by Notani (1938)
First Indian Talkie in English	*Karma* directed by J.L. Freer (1933)
First Talkie house in India	Elphinstone Picture Palace, Calcutta
First International Award – Winner Indian Talkie	*Sant Tukaram* adjudged the best Film of the Year in the Fifth International Film Exhibition at Venice 1937

(*Adapted from an Indian list, publication untraceable*)

CHAPTER 2

The Distinctiveness of Indian Popular Cinema

A distinction needs to be drawn between the 'popular' and the 'artistic' traditions of filmmaking in India. Popular films are the films seen and appreciated by the vast mass of Indian movie-goers. They are largely melo-dramatic, often musicals, conveying simple clear moral messages; they represent a distinctly Indian approach to cinema as a form of mass entertainment. The artistic films, which constitute only about ten per cent of the total output, are realistic, often inspired by neo-realism, and seek to capture a segment of Indian reality. These are the kinds of films that are shown at international film festivals in London, Paris, Berlin, Venice, Tokyo and Toronto. Internationally acclaimed filmmakers such as Satyajit Ray, Mrinal Sen, Ritwik Ghatak, Adoor Gopalakrishnan work in the artistic tradition. There are thus very clear differences in terms of theme, style and technique between the two streams of filmmaking in India.

It is in popular cinema that we see most vividly the 'Indianness' of Indian cinema. In terms of the exploration of complex and multifaceted human experiences, depth of psychological motivation and social vision, popular films may be found wanting. However, in terms of popular response and how popular imagination is shaped, they are highly significant. With their unique combination of fantasy, action, song, dance and spectacle, Indian popular films constitute a distinctively Indian form of mass entertainment.

There are a number of genres associated with Indian popular cinema. Most significant are: mythological films with the fantastic narrations of ancient stories; devotional films that foreground the diverse forms of union with divinity; romantic films dealing with erotic passion as they confront social conventions; stunt films where the focus is on the action and physicality;

historical films with fanciful stage settings and costumes, social films that explore important social problems and issues; and family melodramas that seek to explore tensions and upheavals within the matrix of the family. There is nothing specifically Indian about these genres. What is distinctive are the ways in which they have been handled by Indian filmmakers, investing them with a characteristically Indian cultural imprint. Popular films play a central role in the construction of popular Indian consciousness; they are the most dominant and pervasive force responsible for creating in the public mind the notions of heroism, duty, courage, modernity, consumption and glamour. The relationship between Indian popular cinema and modernity is extremely close. Whatever the genre may be, all Indian popular films display a culturally grounded engagement with modernity.

Just as there are a number of significant genres associated with Indian popular cinema, there are a number of significant themes and subjects that find repeated expression. Romantic love, male friendship, motherhood, renunciation, fate, respect for tradition, social injustice are some of the most compelling among them. As with the genres so with the themes – a distinctively culture-specific approach is adopted, giving these Indian films a characteristically Indian outlook. So when examining what is unique about Indian popular cinema we need to pay particular attention to questions of theme and genre.

The Genre of Mythological Films
Mythological films constitute a very important segment of Indian popular cinema. They have their roots in the ancient past in that they deal with characters and events taken from the distant past, very often as inscribed in the epics and scriptures. They depict the actions and interactions of gods, demons and superhuman powers. But they are not merely historical; they portray the interface between the past and the present. The very fact that these traditional stories are presented in a modern and technologised medium like film underlines this. In interesting ways this mythological imagination also informs films based on contemporary experiences. The idea of femininity as represented by Sita and the aspects of alienness and villainy as represented in the image of Ravana are not confined to stories depicting episodes from the *Ramayana* but can also be found in films dealing with modern experiences like *Kartavya* (1985).

The Genre of Devotional Films
One of the best films in this genre is *Sant Tukaram* (1936) directed by V. Damle and S. Fatehlal, which became the first Indian film to win an award

26

at the Venice film festival. It is about a poet-saint who lived in the seventeenth century and who holds the villagers enthralled by his songs of devotion. His wife is somewhat perturbed by his behaviour, and urges him to become more practical and attend to family matters. Tukaram has also to contend with an envious priest and aspiring saint, Salamalo, who hatches various plots against him. Divine intervention results in the saving of Tukaram and the villagers from various catastrophes. As time passes, great leaders come from long distances to sit at the feet of the poet-saint. He is offered wealth and other material blandishments; he rejects them. When the time comes for Saint Tukaram to leave, a divine vehicle is sent for him and he invites his wife to join him. She says she is quite happy with her home and children and she decides to stay on earth. Through a series of intrigues against the low-caste village poet by the high caste temple performer Salamalo, the story is transformed into a memorable film with devotionality at the centre.

The Genre of Social Drama

This genre figured prominently right from the beginning of Indian cinema. What is distinctive about the social dramas is the way that social issues are treated with a characteristically Indian flavour cinematically. *Achut Kanya*, made in 1936, is an early exploration of an important social issue that had been highlighted by leaders such as Gandhi and Nehru. The film deals with the love between a Brahmin boy and an untouchable girl. They cannot unite – caste and religious barriers stand in their way. The Brahmin boy is compelled to marry someone he does not love and the girl is similarly forced into a marriage with someone she dislikes. They happen to meet at a village fair. The girl's husband, insane with jealousy, misconstrues this meeting and attacks his wife's former friend. They fight on a level-crossing. A train comes down the track. The girl tries to separate the two men and is run over and killed. Through this tragedy, the filmmakers call attention to the problem of untouchability. In most of these social dramas with a clear social message, the action unfolds within a framework of melodrama. This is also true of recent films in this genre.

For example, Mani Rathnam's film, *Bombay* (1995) generated a great deal of interest and controversy, both within and outside India. It explores a highly sensitive issue – relations between Hindus and Muslims in India. The film deals with the love between a young Hindu man, a journalist, and a young Muslim woman. Initially, both their families are strongly against their union. They flee to Bombay and get married. They have two children. Later their families are won over to the marriage. Just as things begin to look up for the couple, the fierce and bloody clashes between Hindus and Muslims erupt in the city of Bombay. Director Mani Rathnam has highlighted the self-defeating nature of extremist thinking and xenophobia and stressed the need to take a more rational approach to the whole question of religious loyalties and ethnic affiliations in the context of multiracial, multi-religious India. Once again the story unfolds within the framework of melodrama.

The Erotic/Romantic Genre

Romance and eroticism have always featured strongly in Indian popular cinema. As with most traditions of cinema in the East and the West, romantic films are extremely popular in India and have been so from the very beginning of Indian cinema. Here again, one sees very clearly the shaping hand of culture. Unlike in Western films, overt sexuality is prohibited in Indian films, so much is conveyed through suggestion, innuendo, coded signs and symbols. Songs and dances play a crucial role, eroticism and sexuality often being closely linked with song and dance numbers. In these romantic films, the sentiments expressed and the ways of expression are rooted in traditional culture. Indian film historians observe that in order to understand the true meaning of Indian romantic films we need to reconnect them with tradition. In this regard, the 'Laila-Majnu' and 'Radha-Krishna' traditions are important. In the 'Laila-Majnu' tradition, love is seen as the essential desire of God; earthly love is regarded as a preparation for heavenly love. The absolute devotion of the woman to the man, marital fidelity, loving secretly but without guilt are important aspects of this tradition. The 'Radha-Krishna' tradition, on the other hand, emphasises the here and the now, the desire to capture the joy of each moment as it passes. Love is seen not as tragic but as tender and joyous. In some popular films such as *Barsaat* (Rain, 1949) and *Andaaz* (Imagination, 1949) both traditions are present. This brief discussion of the different genres that go to form popular Indian cinema indicates the importance of reading the cultural inscriptions found in each. It is these cultural inscriptions that give Indian popular cinema its distinctive flavour.

Characterisation

In Indian popular cinema, there are a number of readily identifiable characters who already have specific valuations attached to them. The hero, heroine, villain, comic are commonly found in Indian cinema as well as in most other popular cinema. However, in Indian cinema there are a few characters who are distinctly Indian in outlook both in their conception and in the role they play in propelling the story. The figure of the mother is the most important. She is crucial in the epic, the *Mahabharata* and many classical mythological stories and folk tales. Drawing on these resources also, modern Indian filmmakers have constructed an image of the mother that is highly visible in Indian cinema. She is caring, steadfast in her devotion to the family, nurturing and upholding moral values. A common image is of her praying in the temple or at home and she epitomises the virtues of religiosity and spirituality. At times the mother finds herself in very difficult situations, caught as she is between competing loyalties. For example, in the popular film *Deewar* (The Wall, 1975) the mother is torn between her love for her immoral son and the imperatives of morality and lawfulness. This film deals with the interactions of two brothers – one a smuggler, played by Amitabh Bachchan, and the other a police officer, played by Shashi Kapoor. And the mother is caught in between. In other films, such as *Mother India* (1957), the mother, a hardworking, law-abiding peasant woman, is compelled to shoot her own son when he descends into immorality. We need to pay particular attention to the image of the mother and her distinctiveness, and the kinds of role she plays in the unfolding story (See Thomas, 1989).

Indian popular films are basically morality plays, where good triumphs over evil, and the social order, disrupted by the actions of immoral and villainous people, is restored by the power of goodness. Entertainment and moral edification are combined in a way that has direct appeal to the vast masses of movie-goers and the idea of evil is central in Indian popular filmic discourse. Indian popular films are, as already noted, basically melodramas, and the idea of evil plays a central role in melodramas. As many commentators on melodrama have pointed out, the polarisation between good and bad, the clash between moral and immoral, the antagonism between what is wholesome and what evil is an inescapably dominant ingredient of melodrama. Melodramas by definition deal with characters who are easily recognisable, often stereotypical, and who incarnate the forces of good and evil. Evil is a vital ingredient because melodramas seek to establish the authority of a moral universe. By vanquishing the villain, and the evil he or she embodies, melodramas seek to reassert the moral authority of a world that for a while threatened to fall prey to the dark forces of evil. When we examine Indian popular films this becomes very clear. (For a fuller discussion see Dissanayake, 1993.)

This concept of evil, so central to Indian popular cinema, has been evolving over the years in response to diverse social, cultural and political forces. This is readily illustrated in three of the most well-known popular films: *Kismet* (1943), *Awaara* (1951) and *Sholay* (1975). *Kismet* tells the story of Shekhar, who runs away from home as a child and grows up to be an expert thief. He falls in love with Rani, an ex-dancer who is now almost an invalid, and their relationship fuels the story. *Awaara,* directed by Raj Kapoor and a smash hit

not only in India but in such countries as the former Soviet Union, tells the
story of Judge Raghunath, his wife Bharati, the notorious criminal Jagga, the
judge's son Raj and his girlfriend Rita. Bharati is abducted by Jagga in
revenge for the judge wrongfully convicting him of a crime he did not
commit. Jagga later returns the judge's wife but the news of her abduction
and pregnancy quickly spreads in the community. Upset by this turn of
events, Judge Raghunath decides to discard his wife. In the slums Bharati
gives birth to a son, whom she calls Raj. The film depicts the life of Raj and
the way it relates to his situation. The third film, *Sholay,* is one of the most
popular films ever made in India. *Sholay* can best be described as an
Indianised Western, with the visual vocabulary and the attitudes portrayed in
such films as *The Wild Bunch* (1969) and *The Magnificent Seven* (1962). The
film deals with the lives and conflicts of a group of characters who personify
the pervasiveness of evil in society. Thakur Saheb, a retired police officer and
rural landlord, hires two trigger-happy jailbirds to hunt down a gang of

bandits, led by the much feared Gabbar Singh, who are terrorising villagers. It is interesting to see how in these three films in which the concept of evil is central to the filmic experience, the concept of evil itself has evolved with time and changing circumstances. (For a comprehensive analysis of *Sholay* see Dissanayake and Sahai, 1992.)

Style and Technique

These are as important as the content. Indian popular films are generally melodramatic musicals which are non-naturalistic in the Western sense. The story does not progress in a linear fashion but meanders, with detours and stories within stories. This circular form of narration is commonly found in classical and folk literature. Song, music and dance are significant in conveying the meaning of the story and in generating the desired emotions. Songs fulfil a number of important functions within the filmic experience. They generate emotion; they underline moral messages; they convey eroticism and sexuality whose overt expression is disallowed on the screen; they create the mood for participating in the various episodes. Similarly, dance sequences are important to fulfil a number of different functions. Indian popular films are sometimes referred to contemptuously as 'masalas' (spices). Just as different spices are used in cooking, so the filmmaker, it is contended, uses the standard elements associated with the given formula for success, namely: song, dance, melodrama, stunts, fights, cabaret sequences, exaggerated humour. While there is much substance to this charge, and some of the worst films are nothing but such a formula, the more talented and successful popular filmmakers have deployed these elements with remarkable ingenuity to create a distinctively Indian form of cinema, just as Hong Kong filmmakers have used the styles, techniques and choreography of traditional martial arts to create a distinctively Chinese style of film-making. So when you go to see an Indian popular film, you must do so in the right frame of mind: understand that what you are going to see is not a realistic, western-type film with a linear narrative but a film that conforms to a different set of aesthetic imperatives. (See Thomas, 1985 for a spirited defence of the pleasures and popularity of Indian cinema.)

Until recently, when we talked about Indian popular cinema we meant Hindi films produced in Bombay, and called them 'Bombay Films' or even 'Bollywood'. But this is no longer accurate. A substantial number of popular films are now being produced in the South and in languages such as Tamil and Telugu. Despite the diversity of origin, Indian popular films display readily identifiable characteristics in terms of theme, narrative, style and technique.

Artistic Films

Artistic films differ sharply from popular films. They are realistic, often ethnographic, and they seek to capture important aspects of Indian reality. By and large, they avoid glamour and glitz and use cinema as an artistic medium capable of exploring important areas of Indian experience. They are usually low-budget and are shown at international film festivals. The artistic films, understandably, do not attract the huge audiences that the popular films do. Often they are made in regional languages like Bengali and Malayalam, and do not receive pan-Indian exposure. In terms of the commitment to serious cinema, to making cinema a significant medium of artistic communication, to eschewing the vulgarities and crudities often associated with Indian popular cinema, artistic filmmakers differ significantly from their counterparts in popular cinema.

Satyajit Ray

When we talk of artistic cinema in India the first name that comes up is Satyajit Ray. This is because he was primarily responsible for fashioning this genre and gaining international recognition for it. His film *Pather Panchali*, made in 1955, was the first such film. In a poll conducted in 1992 by the magazine *Sight and Sound*, *Pather Panchali* was voted one of the ten greatest films of all time. It depicts the childhood world of Apu, the little boy whose life and fortunes are recounted in two subsequent films that together form the Apu trilogy. The second film in the trilogy, *Aparajito*, explores the world of Apu from ten to seventeen years of age, and the third, *Apur Sansar*, narrates his marriage and fatherhood against the backdrop of city life in Calcutta. These films offer a striking contrast to Indian popular films. They use understatement effectively, something totally absent in popular films. There is a visual lyricism and a deep humanism that sophisticated cinema lovers the world over find intensely satisfying. Satyajit Ray made a number of significant films in the same mould that have won for him and Indian cinema great international acclaim. His work provides a sense of the preoccupations of artistic cinema and how they differ from popular cinema. Many of Ray's films are readily available in videocassette.

Satyajit Ray is generally regarded as India's greatest filmmaker and, along with Jean Renoir and Vittorio de Sica, he is rated among the great masters of humanist cinema. His film, *Jalsaghar* (The Music Room, 1958) deals with an arrogant member of the declining aristocracy and portrays both his refined taste and ruinous self-indulgence. *Mahanagar* (The Big City, 1963) explores the impact of urbanisation on consciousness and lifestyles. It concerns Arati, a young girl, who decides to take up a job, much against the wishes of some

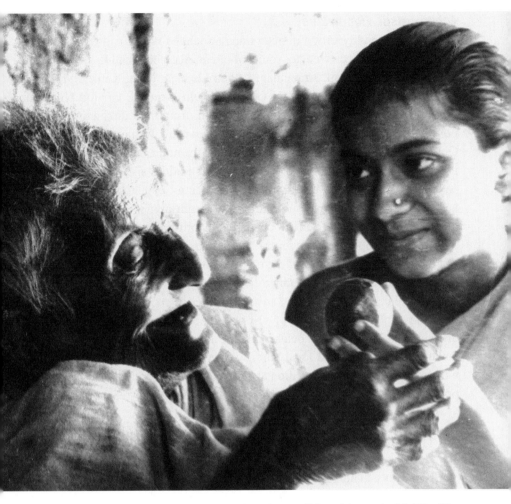

er of the elders in the family, thus disrupting the traditional household. His film
ali Devi (1960) takes as its theme the problem of religiosity and is set in the
1860s. It is about a happy couple who are living in sheltered comfort but who
are tragically engulfed by religious hysteria when the wife is suddenly
thought to be a reincarnation of the goddess Kali. *Charulatha* (1964), which
many consider to be Ray's most accomplished film, is set in Victorian India
and narrates with great sensitivity and cinematic skill the life of a young
woman striving to come to terms with her enforced upper class idleness,
suppressed artistic propensities, and illicit love for her husband's cousin.
Home and the World (1984) similarly explores female subjectivity against a
political background based on a novel by Rabindranath Tagore. Ray's films,
and indeed those of other directors belonging to the artistic tradition, are
clearly quite different from popular films.

Other Artistic Filmmakers

A number of highly gifted directors are associated with the artistic cinema. We have already referred to some of them: Ritwik Ghatak, Mrinal Sen, Adoor Gopalakrishnan, Aravindan, Kumar Shahani, Mani Kaul, Buddhaheb Dasgupta, Aparna Sen, Gautam Ghose, Shyam Benegal, Govind Nihalani, Shaji Karun, Vijaya Mehta, Ketan Mehta. All, from their distinctive vantage points, seek to cinematise important areas of Indian reality. Adoor Gopalakrishnan's film, *Rat Trap* (1981), for example, which has won many prestigious awards, is about Unni the pathetic middle-aged man, unmarried, set in his traditional ways, who cannot accept social change and adjust accordingly. He is demanding and authoritarian and is emblematic of the decaying feudal class. The film charts his inability to adapt to social change and the catastrophic consequences. As in Ray's films, we find remarkable use of understatement, a slow meditative camera that weighs the meaning of the most mundane event, avoiding the flashy exuberance normally associated with popular films. Similarly, in his film *Face to Face* (1984), Gopala-krishnan explores the theme of self and modernisation, this time taking a different angle. The film deals with the love and death of Sreedharan, a devoted Communist and loyal party worker, deeply respected by his fellow workers. He leads the trade union at a tile factory but suddenly begins to shun politics. Once again the style of the film follows the neo-realistic tradition.

As we seek to identify the distinguishing features of Indian cinema, we need to keep in mind the main characteristics of its two main branches – the popular and the artistic. Both relate to the Indian reality and consciousness, but in very different ways. The techniques of popular cinema are largely shaped by traditional narrative, whereas those of the artistic cinema are Western in nature, largely neo-realistic. However, in terms of the experiences explored, the artistic films are much closer to Indian reality than the popular films, which are mostly fantasies. Topics such as self and modernisation, alienation, clash of tradition and modernity and the ensuing confusion of values, Westernisation and its impact, the role of the artist in a consumer society, the subjection of women – issues that are central to a deep understanding of contemporary Indian society – find expression in artistic cinema.

In most artistic films, all aspects of movie-production are deemed ancillary to the presentation of realistic narrative. Hence, camera angles are largely at eye-level; lighting unobtrusive; framing concentrated on the main action of a given scene; cuts effected at logical junctures in the flow of action. Popular cinema, which grew out of different roots, never felt a need to follow this pattern of Western filmmaking. The styles of presentation and techniques associated with popular cinema merit our close attention. Indian popular filmmakers, with their inordinate love for dramatic camera movements, extravagant use of colour, flashy editing, and self-conscious use of sound, depart significantly from the 'invisible' style associated with artistic cinema. Indian popular filmmakers aim to create a different kind of film and narrative discourse. The narrative closure, unobtrusive camera, continuity of image, shot centering, frame balance and sequential editing adopted by artistic film directors sought to create in the minds of the spectator the impression that what is being shown on the screen is an objective reporting of real events rather than a created narrative. Indian popular film directors on the other hand do not conceal the fact that what is on the screen is a creation, an invention by the makers of the film.

This chapter has sought to present in broad outline some of the features that give Indian cinema its distinctiveness. For this purpose we categorised Indian cinema into two groups – the popular and the artistic – and discussed the distinguishing features of each in terms of theme, content, and style. The points we have made in this chapter will become clearer still as we exemplify them in a number of films associated with each group. Indian cinema as it has evolved over the past ninety years is a cinema with a distinctive set of characteristics and it reflects an imaginative world very different from that created by British or French or Italian or Japanese cinema. It is a world that bears the Indian cultural inscription.

Untitled advertisement for a film. India Office file no. L P & J 6 1747, pg.418

PART II

PART II

CHAPTER 3

Cinema and Society in India

Indian cinema is essentially an institution of modernity. This is because it is at one level 'a machine engaged in the mechanical reproduction of images, and so has an impact on the way traditions of representation are refracted through its mechanisms' (Vasudevan, 1995a).

This chapter is divided into two. In the first part we identify the traditions of representation; these are then explored in some depth in the following chapters. In the second part, we examine the economic and institutional paraphernalia associated with the mechanical reproduction of these representations. The primary purpose of this chapter, refracting the traditions of representation/re-presentation, is to focus on entertainment, since cinema is essentially a spectacle. Consequently, issues dealing with the development of an industry geared to mass produce that spectacle for a market will also be explored. Information and discussion of the economics of film production and the relationship between the government and the film industry are not readily available to the general reader but are valuable to our study.

What are the traditions of representation that Indian cinema refracts? India has a long tradition – five thousand years of history, two hundred years as part of the British Empire and only fifty years as an independent country. Conceptualising Indian society is highly problematic. Labels such as Indian and Asian are loosely used. Furthermore, many writers (for example, Varshney, 1993; Kohli, 1990) believe that these are anxious times for India – the decline of the Congress Party and the problems of governability, the assassination of two previous Prime Ministers, the continuing terrorism in the state of Kashmir, the rise of Hindu nationalism and the aggravation of communal violence – yet India has not so far disintegrated as a society. Indeed, it has maintained its national identity and political stability since independence and it is opening up to the world market and is now seen as having much potential for the technological revolution.

Here we focus on those traditions which have a bearing on Indian films and explore how they illuminate the relationship between Indian cinema and Indian society. Two concepts which we regard as central are pluralism and secularism.

The Influence of Religion in Indian Film

India is a religiously plural society – the majority of its people are Hindus. But unlike its 'Christian counterpart where religion is concentrated in churches, religious authority is widely diffused in the Hindu world' (Brown, 1994). Brown notes that the Hindu's religious life is centred on the family and the caste. The church, synagogue or mosque as seats of worship and education have no real Hindu parallel. But who actually is a Hindu? According to Savarkar, father of Hindu nationalism, a Hindu means a person who regards the land from the Indus to the Seas as his fatherland as well as his Holyland.

This definition is territorial (land between the Indus and the Seas), genealogical (fatherland), and religious (holyland). Hindus, Sikhs, Jains and Buddhists can be part of this definition, for they meet all three criteria (Varshney, 1993).

Other minorities – Parsis, Jews and Christians – are assimilated and have become part of the nation's mainstream. Only the Muslims, according to the Hindu nationalists, are the principal adversary, since they are a substantial minority and they have their homeland in Pakistan.

This line of argument, however, marks a significant departure from the idea of nationhood conceived and propagated since Independence. To Nehru and Gandhi, there were no insiders and outsiders in India; throughout its history India has regularly received and accommodated other religions and in this process:

Syncretistic forms of culture and syncretistic forms of religious worship have emerged and become part of India. Religious pluralism in India could not only exist, but also if there was a dispute, the state would maintain a posture of equidistance, a principle that came to define India's secularism (Varshney, 1993:235).

The film *Roja* by Mani Rathnam was one of the most popular in the period 1992-3 and it is generally considered to be extraordinarily well made (it was awarded the President's National Integration Award). As the review by

Niranjana (1994) indicates, *Roja* is a text about nationalism, the power of the state and the future of secularism.

The film is set in Kashmir against a backdrop of terrorism. Rishi Kumar, a young scientist, is kidnapped and held captive by terrorists in retaliation for the capture of their leader by Indian security forces. His wife struggles for her husband's release and ultimately succeeds. But what the film does is to point out through the hero the misguided action of the Kashmiri separatists, since Kashmir is part of India. Nevertheless, Mani Rathnam does present the human face of the terrorists and is careful to avoid siding with either the Hindus or the Muslims. *Roja* highlights the centrality of the question of national integration; the story wavers dramatically between the hero's invocations of *Jai Hind* (long live India!) and the cost of being beaten senseless and the bond that developed between the captive and the terrorists.

It is partly in response to the disintegrative tendency of the Kashmir (Muslim) separatists that the Hindutva's commitment to India's territorial integrity can be understood. As Varshney (1993) says 'Most of India is, and has been, Hindu by religion – anywhere between 65 and 70 per cent in the early twentieth century and 82 per cent today'. Consequently, it would be fruitful to state in a summarised form what Hindus believe and then focus on the beliefs and traditions as they are reflected in and refracted through the cinema.

Hinduism

According to Bruce (1995: 84-85) the term 'Hindu' simply means 'of India'. As one would expect, given the size of the Indian subcontinent and the ethnic and linguistic diversity of those who have inhabited it, Hinduism is extraordinarily complex and encompasses almost every possible sort of religious belief and practice, from pagan superstition to ascetic and scholarly traditions.

The heart of the philosophical Hinduism of the Brahmans is *dharma* which, at the cosmic level, means 'self-subsistence', that which has no antecedent cause, and is comparable to the Christian 'Word'. As it says at the start of John's gospel: 'In the beginning was the Word, and the Word was with God and the Word was God'. *Dharma* also means 'universal law' or norm, which applies at the moral, the ritual, and the social levels. Every individual has a *dharma* specific to his/her social status and stage of life. There is also a *dharma* specific to each caste.

As in Buddhism, the individual's spirit (or *Atma*) is thought to be 'really' just an embodiment of the universal soul but, in so far as it has an identity, it is retained through a series of reincarnations.

Underlying reincarnation and everything else is *karma*, which means both action and the consequences of actions. Rebirth is a profoundly moral process in that the accumulation of good *karma* will ensure a better birth next time round. This doctrine is, not surprisingly, favoured by high-caste Brahmans because it explains their privileges as being deserved by their good actions in previous lives and it reconciles the lower orders to their humble position.

The good Hindu life has four ends. In addition to *dharma*, there is *artha* (correct behaviour in the material world of productive and economic activity) and *kama* (the pursuit of love and pleasure). Proper action in these spheres will lead to the fourth end: *moksha* or release from the cycle of rebirth. As in the Buddhist tradition, the culmination of religious activity is final departure from the material world.

There is no single work or canon which contains the authoritative version of divine revelation. Instead of a Pentateuch, Bible or Quran, there are a very large number of sources. The Vedas, the oldest of which date back to 3000 BC, contain hymns, ritual instructions, and philosophical observations. Then there are the two great epics: the *Ramayana* and the *Mahabarata*. The latter tells the story of a great battle in which Prince Arjuna is taught the significance of *dharma* by the God Krishna, who acts as his charioteer. The convoluted story shows the dreadful consequences which result when people follow their own interpretation of duty rather than that laid down by Krishna and teaches that the highest morality lies in doing what has to be done, entirely detached from the consequences.

The Hindu text best known in the West, the *Bhagavad Gita*, is an excerpt from the *Mahabarata* and illustrates the connection between *dharma* and *karma*. Brahmanic Hinduism is complemented by a theistic devotional strand which worships, among many others, Indra (God of Rain), Surya (Sun), Chandra (Moon), Ganesha (the remover of obstacles, depicted as a creature with four arms and an elephant's head), Yama (death), Sarasvati (Goddess of learning and wife of Brahma), and Lakshmi (Goddess of wealth and wife of Vishnu).

The philosophical strand readily encompasses the theistic cults by supposing that the variety of deities are 'really' illusory embodiments of the single spirit of cosmic consciousness. They provide a useful channel for the religious consciousness of the less sophisticated, in the same way that the cult of Mary provides a way to God for the less sophisticated Catholic.

Central to an understanding of Hinduism, as the summary above which we have adapted from Bruce (1995) indicates, is the immense variety of beliefs and practices which form part of the 'Great Tradition', because its roots are in textual religious sources and in the laws of such classical ethical codes as *Manusmriti*. However, the main sources of the Hindu tradition are the two epics, the *Mahabharata* and the *Ramayana* which have informed and influenced Indian cinema since its beginnings. Consequently, we offer a summary of the essential points of these epics.

The *Mahabharata* revolves around the struggles between two princely families, the Pandavas and their cousins, the Kauravas for possession of a kingdom located near the present city of Delhi. The central character of the epic is Lord Krishna, a man of action and a statesman. The climax is the great battle in which Lord Krishna becomes the charioteer of Arjuna, one of the Pandava brothers. The lengthy conversation between them is the subject matter of the *Bhagavad Gita*, which is in many ways the most important aspect of the narrative. For although the Pandavas were victorious, the story of the struggles occupies only about a quarter of the epic, the rest being devoted to Indian philosophical, metaphysical, spiritual and ethical thinking.

The *Ramayana* is shorter than the *Mahabharata* and celebrates the life and exploits of Rama. Prince Rama is exiled by his father for fourteen years at the behest of Rama's step-mother Kaikeji. He leaves with his wife Sita and brother Lakshman. While in the forest, Sita is kidnapped by the demon-king, Ravana of Lanka. Rama, helped by an army of monkeys led by Hanuman, regains her and his kingdom of Ayodhya.

The influence of these two epics in the lives of Indians and on Indian popular cinema cannot be overestimated. The *Mahabharata* embodies the Hindu understanding of the concept of *dharma*. This is what sustains world order. From the *Mahabharata* people learn the rules and the codes of ideal conduct laid down for everybody. It is an encyclopaedia of Indian culture and has been described as the National Epic of India.

Likewise, stories from the *Ramayana* are constantly told and retold and through them people learn the difference between right and wrong, develop a high sense of values and understand what constitutes ideal behaviour. Rama himself is the epitome of all the virtues, an example to all people of honour, courage and loyalty. One of the most important themes in the *Ramayana* is the potential in all human beings for good and evil. The destruction of evil by good, either by oneself or by divine intervention, is a constant theme of Hinduism and of Indian popular cinema.

While much has been written about the influence of the *Mahabharata* and the *Ramayana* on Phalke, father of the Indian film industry – for example his *Lanka Dahan* (The Burning of Lanka, 1917) is taken from a significant episode from the *Ramayana* – recent directors such as Shyam Benegal and Kumar Shahani have also explicitly drawn upon the epics. For example, Benegal's *Kalyug* (Dark Age, 1981) and Shahani's *Tarang* (Wave, 1984)

use structural and thematic elements from the great Indian epic, the *Mahabharata*, for a modern retelling of the ancient narrative of familial enmity, opposition and self-destruction. The epic provides the framework for a dramatic representation of power and greed in the business world of contemporary India (Chakravarty, 1996:253).

The Relationship Between Cinema and Society

The Role of the Family

We can explore the role of the mother in three films: *Mother India* (1957), *Deewar* (The Walls, 1975) and *Ram Lakhan* (Lord Ram and Lakshman, 1989). In all three, the story revolves around a lone woman bringing up her sons in hostile circumstances. But the ways in which each faces and fights those circumstances demonstrate the changes in Indian society over the past three decades. As observed by Geetha (1990), the picture of Nargis, the mother in *Mother India* is a humanistic one, if politically naive. In *Deewar*, the mother (Nirupa Roy) is less sturdy and withdraws into the world of 'pujas' and prayers – thus becoming marginalised. This theme is further developed in *Ram Lakhan*, where the mother (Rakhee) waits seventeen years for her sons to grow up and avenge her indignities.

The status of the mother and her relationship with her children are interesting. In *Mother India*, the mother does not depend on her husband; in *Deewar* she is defined as a widow towards the end of the film and invested with the traditional signs of Indian widowhood. In *Ram Lakhan*, the mother is already a widow and the 'only justification for her existence after her husband's death seems to be her desire for revenge' (Geetha, 1990:10).

It is fascinating to examine the model of ideal Indian womanhood reflected and refracted through the changing role of both the mother in Indian films and the Indian family in Indian society. The role of the mother is clearly invested with the spiritual qualities of self sacrifice, devotion and religiosity. Right from the earliest Indian films, for example in *Raja Harischandra* (1913), the role of the daughters of India was steadily defined. 'They were to be obedient daughters, self-sacrificing mothers and devoted wives, defined by their relationship to men or to patriarchal social structures' (Geetha, 1990:13).

a   A number of writers (Chatterjee, 1993; Arnold and Hardiman, 1994) have shown how this construction of motherhood and womanhood is central to the colonial discourse on women and how it forms part of the wider processes operating in the world of capitalist social relations beyond Britain and India.

What about the construction of the family itself? Illumination can be found in the 1994 film *Hum Aapke Hain Koun* (HAHK – who am I to you?) which achieved considerable commercial success and has been compared to such blockbusters as *Sholay* (1975) and *Mughal-e-Azam* (1960). At the seminar on Popular Culture in India at the School for Oriental and African Studies (SOAS) in June 1995, Uberoi presented an illuminating paper on the film *HAHK* and we draw upon this here.

There are a number of surprising elements about *HAHK*. It is a modest budget family drama without the 'masala' ingredients of sex, sadism and violence so characteristic of recent 'Bollywood' films. It has a considerable number of melodious songs and catchy tunes, but no more than *Roja* (1992) or *1942: A Love Story* (1994). What is most surprising is that it is a 'clean family movie'. In describing the film as clean and morally uplifting, Uberoi has drawn attention to a number of themes in the film, including the following:

a) **The family as tradition**. There is consensus among viewers that HAHK is about not only joint family but also Indian culture and tradition. The possible break-up of the Indian joint family system due to processes of urbanisation, industrialisation and westernisation has been causing concern for the past fifty years. However, the film is more about what the family should be rather than what it is; hence, there is no antagonism between the father figure and the sons, for example, no tension between the brothers and no tension between mother-in-law and daughter-in-law. Perhaps the best comment comes from Madhuri Dixit, who won the filmfare award for Best Actress of 1994: 'Hum Aapke Hain Koun presents a perfect 'utopia' – about simple values and guileless people'.

b) **Vulgarity.** Sex and vulgarity have been part and parcel of all popular cinema since it began. Indian cinema has had its fair share, but in recent years the Indian public has witnessed more of it through satellite and cable TV channels. Uberoi claims that an important aspect of *HAHK* as a 'family' film is that the whole family (grandparents, parents and children) can watch it together without embarrassment. Despite its highly simplified structure, the film is a universal love story but, as Uberoi rightly suggests, 'the conflicts in the film are those between *dharma* (duty) and desire and between freedom and destiny – conflicts which have to be reconciled before a love story can come to a satisfactory happy ending'.

But perhaps the most important aspect of *HAHK* is how it reinforces India's cultural heritage through depicting series of rituals – betrothal, engagement, the *mehndi* (the decoration of the bride's hands with leaves of the Henna), marriage ceremonies and the celebration of the new-born child. Indeed, according to Uberoi, 'the most remarkable instance is the marriage ceremony itself, the centre-piece and indeed the *raison d'être* of the movie'.

Hindi films are seen as 'collective fantasies' since they have many features in common with fairy tales. Like fairy tales, Hindi films have the psychological function of producing a sense of security by upholding the picture of a world in which the family and *dharma* are safe (Kakar mentioned in Valicha, 1988:35) and that there are parallels between the Hindi film and certain popular myths.

The Role of Language in Hindi Films

How do films communicate the collective fantasies which, according to Kakar, characterise Indian popular cinema? Language has a significant bearing on the relationship between cinema and society in India. Adequate and appropriate communication is possible only through the languages of the people, their mother tongues and, as Oomen (1990:131-132) rightly notes, the polyglot character of the Indian nation-state renders the challenge particularly stupendous: 'we are here referring to 800 million people, one-sixth of humanity'.

A conservative estimate puts the number of languages in India at over 100. However, the Indian constitution recognises only 15 major languages, with Hindi spoken by about 40 per cent of the population. Consequently, although the South of India is more prolific in terms of film production – in Tamil, Telugu, Malayalam and Kannada – and, although Calcutta is normally seen to lead the rest of India as a centre for quality, the grip of Bombay with its emphasis on Hindi is tighter. In 1993, films in Hindi numbered only 182 out of over 800 but they cater to 'the all-Indian market and are understood by the majority of the Indian population (an achievement in India's polylingual society for which the Bombay film itself has claimed its fair share of credit)' (Chakravarty, 1996:9).

The subject and treatment of popular Hindi films are tried, trusted and predictable – a planned mixture of stars, songs, dances and titillation – the story is just a peg on which to hang these elements. The stars themselves (and their ratings) are the most important aspect of any film – they are sought after and relentlessly pursued: Amitabh Bachchan, Sanjay Dutt, Salman Khan, Sharukh Khan, Madhuri Dixit.

Until the 1970s, love stories were very popular and in India, where arranged marriages are still common, Indian films have created a new legitimacy for love-marriage through various devices. According to Nandy (1981), the best-known devices include the following:

a) the couple discover that their parents had planned to get them married to each other anyway.

b) the hero, separated from the heroine by barriers of caste, status or wealth, does a good turn to the girl's family, so that the family, in the last scene, guiltily give their girl in marriage to him as a reward

c) alternatively, it is the heroine who does a good turn to win the hearts of the hero's arrogant family.

Another strategy of Indian narrative structure is the double roles, particularly with regard to the main male protagonists – often two sons, one good and the other bad, one meek and the other aggressive. Sometimes it is the 'lost-'n'-found', 'cops and robbers' formulae with crime being the fulcrum for all kinds of plots.

Scenes of Violence

Many critics have commented on the gratuitous scenes of violence and gory deaths which have characterised the Indian popular cinema since the 1970s. This period saw the rise of Amitabh Bachchan as the 'angry young man' who went on to become the last of the superstars and, according to the Indian press, 'a colossus who may not be seen again'. It marked a decisive break with the past. Any love triangle occupies a secondary position; in many of the films of the 1970s and early 1980s, hero Bachchan has little time for speeches. Using his height and his voice to full advantage, he concentrated on what the plot required him to do – generally to settle a score or redress an injustice. Violence reached its apogee in *Sholay* (Flames, 1975) a film which has become a legend. Bachchan was no longer the avenger seeking justice but a mercenary, selling his prowess as a killer, for a price (Garga, 1996:184). One of the most noticeable features of *Sholay* is that while the two heroes (Bachchan and Dharmendra) still value friendship and male bonding (*dosti*), there is no regard for family values (see Dissanayake and Sahai, 1992 for a cultural reading of *Sholay*).

We said at the beginning of this chapter that the cinema refracts the traditions of representation. One reason for the enormous success of these Amitabh Bachchan films is that the 1970s were a period of deep crisis in India. There was urban crime, spiralling inflation, corrupt and sectarian politics – to such an extent that Mrs Gandhi, then Prime Minister, imposed a State of Emergency in 1975. Out of the window went the kind of romanticism associated with Rajesh Khanna, for example. The public was looking for a hero to put things right and Amitabh Bachchan fitted the bill perfectly.

But Amitabh Bachchan's films did not eliminate the significance of music and dance. According to Barnouw and Krishnaswamy (1963), music is an integral element of Indian film – its importance is due to the structure of Indian traditional performance. Indeed, 'classical Sanskrit theatre made no separation between the arts of music, song and dance – all were required for a perfect enactment of the performance themes, whether they were sacred or secular in nature' (Beeman, 1981). We devote a sub-section to the importance of the role of music, song and dance in Indian cinema later in this book. Here, it is sufficient to identify some of the aspects of music, song and dance in Indian cinema.

In a paper for a Postgraduate Seminar at the Institute of Commonwealth Studies in 1991, Kabir outlined the development of Indian Film music from its early days until 1991. She drew attention to how, ever since the introduction of sound in *Alam Ara* (1931), films became dependent 'on the song in a way that has differentiated Indian cinema from most world cinema'. Remember that *Indrasabha* (The Court of Lord Indra) produced in 1932 had 70 songs!

How the songs were sung changed. In the early thirties and forties, the songs were recorded live during the filming of the song sequence and the 'song would be picturised in a single take, which meant that the song sequence would be virtually static' (Kabir, 1991:1). Since the 1950s, playback singing has become an established feature of music production and this has produced a host of playback singers, including Mukesh, Rafi, Lata Mangeshkar, Kishore Kumar, Kumar Shanu, Udit Narayan, Kavita Krishnamurthy and Alka Yagnik, many of whom have achieved international reputation in their own right.

Dance is equally important in Indian films. Sanskrit theatre integrated dance music and acting – *Natya* and *Sangeet* – separation only recently has occurred. Dance is an inseparable aspect of Indian culture and is manifested in all Indian festivals and religious occasions. Classical dancing was originally associated with the Devdasis in the south and with the Kothivalis in the north. Many men dancers were eunuchs and the dancing women could not lead normal lives. The dance of the eunuchs and of the Kothivalis was called *Nautch*.

Through a mixture of dance forms from the West and other parts of the world, the Indian film industry has popularised and liberated Indian dance from its low status. In 1948, the costliest and most spectacular film of the period, *Chandralekha*, dramatically changed the nature of film production. Nearly three and a half hours long, the film culminated in a spectacular dance which later film producers tried to emulate but never equalled.

The Economics of the Film Industry and the State

Filmmaking is very costly. In the beginning, Indian films were financed from sources connected with the film industry, both the distribution and exhibition sectors contributing to the making of films. By the time of the Second World War, the film industry had, in the words of Majumdar (1995:301), 'a look of solidarity and self respect and among the Indian industries, cinema occupied the 8th place reckoned in terms of investment in the early forties'.

However, the Indian film business has never been officially considered an industry, so raising money from financial institutions has always been problematic. This, coupled with the high rate of failures at the box office, particularly in recent years, has made the financing of films very risky.

The Second World War created a boom in the film industry which, because it had no standardised practices, provided fertile ground for people with 'hot money'. This led, according to Majumdar (1995), to the decline of the studio system, where actors and crew were employees, and the rise of the star system, with stars becoming freelance artists who performed in more than one film at a time. Consequently, the star, the music director and the playback singer became the beneficiaries of the new order (p.302).

Meanwhile, the import of foreign films was, until 1957, allowed freely through Indian importers as well as some foreign companies. In 1960, the government established the Film Finance Corporation (FFC) and in the middle of the 1960s, an informal system of canalisation of films through the State Trading Corporation was introduced; subsequently, the National Film Development Corporation (NFDC) replaced the FFC and canalised the import of feature films, but this ceased in 1992.

The government's casual approach to the film industry is evident from the fact (reported by Majumdar, 1995) that there are no reliable data on such basic information as the total capital invested in the film industry in India, the annual investment in filmmaking gross collections or the sources from which production is obtained. Very little research has been carried out in this rather nebulous but extremely important area. *The Economics of Film Industry in India* (Jain, 1960) provided an overview of the field. Jain examined matters such as the technology of filmmaking, the raw materials and equipment required, as well as wages and welfare issues. He also provided useful information on the average costs of films, marketing and taxation and some international comparisons. Though limited in scope – it provided very little information on the exhibitions and their interrelationship with the producers and distributors – the book is a landmark.

Dharap's *Indian Films* provides extensive statistical information on various aspects of the film industry such as the number of cinema halls, the number of films produced in India and estimated costs of film production. First published in 1973, subsequent volumes (1974, 1975, 1977, 1979 and 1985) are 'only statistical updates'. In *Economics of Indian Cinema*, Oomen and Joseph (1991) deal with Malayalam films only, but in their introduction and in chapter two they give a useful overview of the commercialisation of the film industry in India. Recently, however, Mital's (1995) *Cinema Industry in India* focuses primarily on pricing and taxation, and he too notes that the 'economics of entertainment is a highly under-researched area of study' and that literature on this subject is 'scant and academic works are few and far between.'

Maitra's (1995) *100 years of Cinema* offers a useful summary of the cinema-going public and India's cinemas. He asserts that India has a cinema-going population of 65 million per week, though the cinemas number about 13,000 of which 6,500 are permanent and the rest touring. This works out to seven seats per thousand of the population, a very low rate compared to other large countries and considering that they are spread over 22 states and nine union territories. Half of the theatres are in the South.

Film budgets range between 3 crores (Rs30,000,000 i.e. about £540,000) and 6 lakhs (Rs600,000 i.e. about £11,000), the multi-star spectacle 'standing at one extreme end – the shoestring art and realism saga at the other!'. A moderately successful film earns much more than its costs and various outlets which have recently opened up have created new avenues for revenue, like the video market at home and overseas, audio rights, telecast on Doordashan (the National Television system) and various satellite TV channels.

So why do people go to the movies? Until the arrival of television, cinema-going was a regular and habit-forming part of people's lives all over the world. The excitement, the novelty and the entertainment which the technology of film production provided had no parallel in people's lives. For the young, cinema halls were places of romance where young people could get together secretly, sheltered by the relative anonymity of the crowd and the dark environment. There were (and still are) films which catered for the gratification of urban youth culture.

Cinema-going was (and to some extent still is) also part of family entertainment. The impact of these social occasions on the lives of people is under researched, but it is clear from a number of interviews carried out, particularly for television programmes – for example the one by Munni Kabir for her programme Movie Mahal on Channel 4 – that many people remember their childhood visits to the cinema in the company of their parents. As they grew up, many saw films which, according to their parents and the Board of Censors, they should not have seen. Consequently, at some stage in the lives of the vast majority of people, cinema-going was almost an act of transgression against parental authority.

The Movie Moguls

Who are these moguls who built cinema halls and financed the industry? The situation in India is different from that in the West. With the arrival of television in the West in the 1950s and 1960s, cinema attendance dropped and many cinemas closed down. However, in recent years, the film industry has fought back with blockbusters such as *Jurassic Park*. In India, however, television is not yet widespread; consequently, cinema attendance has so far not suffered materially. It is true that satellite, cable and video facilities are having an impact on the cinema-going public, but they seem to have made this public more discriminating. Cinema-going is still far more important to people than television.

The earlier movie moguls operated in the studio system. Garga (1996) documents the activities of some of the better known – J. F. Madhan of the Elphinstone Company, Chandulal Shah of Ranjit Movietone, B. N. Sircar, Devaki Bose, P.C. Barua, Nitin Bose of New Theatres, Damle, Fatehlal and Shantaram of Prabhat Studio and Himansu Rai of Bombay Talkies. But there is little reliable information on the financial entrepreneurs of recent decades. Das Gupta (1991:268) asserts that 'the finance for these films comes largely from a parallel economy lying outside the pale of the legitimate organised sector of banking and insurance and manufacturing industries'. Recent reports by the press are disturbing. Producer Mukesh Duggal was gunned down at Andheri, allegedly for refusing to give extortion money. The Dawood Ibrahim gang is reported to be increasingly targeting Hindi film producers and financiers for extortion money and the situation has deteriorated to such an extent that certain producers have fled abroad. According to the *Financial Times* of 13 August (1997: 6), Gulshan Kumar, India's 'Cassette King' and a movie mogul was shot dead, reportedly by Bombay gangsters. *The Financial Times* comments that 'Bombay's thriving movie industry has long had connections with organised crime, largely through the laundering of 'black' money used to finance many of the all-singing, all-dancing Hindi musicals which make Bollywood the world's most prolific film capital'.

Film Censorship

If the operations of the movie moguls are not always transparent, those of the government with regard to film censorship are quite clear. During colonial times, the British rulers were determined that cinema should serve their colonial policy. In the early years of Indian cinema, vigorous attempts were made by the rulers to regulate cinema for a variety of reasons, chief among them the desire to preserve the 'prestige of the white woman'. Constance

Bromley, former secretary and manager of the Opera House in Calcutta, a premier picture house, wrote an inflammatory newspaper article upon her return to England headlined: 'Films That Lower Our Prestige in India: Imperilling the Prestige of the White Woman' (quoted by Arora, 1995).

As the influence of the British began to decline in India, cinema was credited with spreading communism. According to the author of a classified report *The Cinema in the East: Factors in the Spread of Communism* (quoted by Arora, 1995)

...there can be no doubt that the way for Communist influence has been greatly facilitated by a powerful and novel element, which in recent years has entered into the lives of semi-civilized people in all parts of the tropical world. That element is the cinema.

Arora (1995:47) comments perceptively:

It is chronic that whereas the native was believed incapable of compre-hending such genres of American cinema as romantic comedy or social parody, s/he was nevertheless credited with comprehending the narrative of such Soviet films as *Battleship Potemkin* and *Ivan the Terrible* and consequently being swayed by 'Communist propaganda'.

All these factors help to explain why, half a century after the departure of the British, Indian cinema is still one of the most heavily censured. The Film Censor Board of India continues 'to impose restrictions on the depiction of adult sexuality in a weak, though desperate, attempt at maintaining an essentialist and nationalistic distinction between western and Indian character types' (Arora, 1995:48). The Indian film industry subverts this control mainly through its song and dance sequences.

But here, too, things are changing. Recent developments are discussed in Chapter 7.

CHAPTER 4
Religion, Ethnicity and Caste in Indian Cinema

India is a multi-ethnic, multi-lingual and multi-religious society. Questions of religion, language and ethnicity play a significant part in the lives of the people, often generating tensions and acrimony. In addition, there is the question of caste, a distinguishing feature of the Hindu social order. As issues of caste, ethnicity and religion meet contemporary modernising forces, a sense of confrontation naturally emerges. These vital social issues find expression in Indian cinema. As we have argued, cinema both reflects and shapes society and Indian films have mirrored the religious, ethnic and caste tensions in society and also intervened in debates related to them, so shaping the discussion. This chapter looks at religious divisions, ethnic and caste conflicts and how enlightened film directors in India are seeking to create a better understanding of these issues.

The rather elusive nature of the concepts of religion, ethnicity and caste adds to the complexity. Accordingly, we try to clarify the terms and some relevant details so that their pertinence to Indian cinema can be understood.

Religion and Indian Popular Cinema
There are many religions in India, including Hinduism, Islam, Christianity, Buddhism and Jainism but the vast majority of Indian films that have a religious theme are Hindu in outlook. D.J. Phalke, the originator of Indian cinema, based his first feature film, *Raja Harischandra*, on a Hindu religious story, after he saw a film about the life of Christ. We noted how Indian filmmakers were from the start drawn to the *Ramayana* and the *Mahabharata* for stories, characters, ethos and values and this still continues. Religion and cinema are inseparably linked in Indian culture. However, religion in India is a highly sensitive issue and, according to Madan (1989),

'to write about it without querying the idea of religion as a discrete element of everyday life is to yield to the temptation of words'.

To what extent is an understanding of the religious traditions of India necessary to an appreciation of its cinema? We concentrate on the dominant religion, Hinduism, since Hindu religious traditions and practices mark the content, structure and dominant moods of Indian films generally. The relationship of Hinduism to Islam in particular and its impact on the film industry and the content of films needs also to be understood.

Sanatana Dharma – The Eternal Law

The eternal law governs the evolution of the individual from conception to death and to live in harmony with the laws of Nature herself. The traditional vision of life is holistic and this is the first principle for any understanding of religion in India. This vision of life encompasses almost every kind of religious belief and practice from pagan superstitions to scholarly traditions. However, some of the core concepts of Hinduism can be identified. These concepts include *karma, dharma, maya*, rebirth and renunciation.

As we noted earlier, at the heart of Hinduism is *dharma* – the Cosmic Moral Social order. The *Mahabharata* (C.400 BC – 400 AD) says '*Dharma* is so called because it protects *dharmat* (everything). *Dharma* maintains everything that has been created; *dharma* is thus that very principle which can maintain the universe' (Madan, 1989). This is comparable to the Christian 'Word', as in the Biblical: 'In the beginning was the Word, and the Word was with God and the Word was God'. There is, however, a significant difference in the ontological assumptions, since Hindus never contemplated the universe as a perfect system, governed by general laws.

Dharma, then, is a metaphysical concept, embracing as it does the abstract principle of the social order. It has, however, practical consequences – namely, 'the obligation and the tendency to act in a particular way in specified situations. The synthesis of thought and practice is even more clearly expressed in the notion of *karma*' (Madan, 1989: 122) – every action has its inevitable consequences. A person's life is determined by the good deeds and the bad deeds that s/he has performed in previous lives.

The concept of *karma* is closely linked to the idea of rebirth and seeks to explain the sufferings and hardships that one has to encounter in everyday life. Although the concept of *karma*, as enunciated in classical Indian texts, is highly complex, touching on philosophical and moral issues in the popular mind, it has been simplified to mean that some people are rich and others are poor, some people are healthy and others are not, because of their *karma*, their past deeds. The concept of *dharma*, as formulated in traditional texts, is equally complex and deals with issues of social order, law, religious sanctions, morality, duties and obligations and so on. However, in the popular imagination it has been simplified to mean the maintenance of the social order and the acceptance of one's prescribed life and the performance of one's duties accordingly. The notion of *maya*, as understood by the public and as portrayed in Indian films, is that the world is illusory. A veil is drawn between human beings and reality, and that veil constitutes *maya*. This is again tied to the concepts of *samsara* and *moksha* (liberation). So long as human beings fail to realise that the phenomenal world is illusory and that there is a deeper and real world of the inner self, they will be caught in the never-ending cycle of rebirth and fail to achieve liberation. The idea of rebirth is central to the Hindu view of life. Human beings are born again and again until they realise the deeper reality of life. The human soul remains the same, but it takes on and discards many bodily shapes. As the famous Hindi text, the *Bhagavad Gita*, states:

As a man casts off his worn-out clothes
And takes on other new ones in their place,
So does the embodied soul cast off his worn-out bodies
And enters others new.

The idea of renunciation is also central to the Hindu view of life and finds expression in many Indian films. According to the Hindus, there are four stages in a person's life. First a student, second a householder, third a hermit and fourth a holy man or one who has renounced worldly life for the quest of truth. Renunciation is thus a highly prized virtue. Watching Indian films with these concepts in mind enables us to understand the intentions of the filmmakers better and also the deeper layers of meanings embedded in the narratives.

Religious Explicitness

The relationship of these key concepts of Hinduism to Indian cinema can be studied at different levels. Firstly, there are films which are explicitly religious in nature, drawing their stories from religious sources, most notably the *Mahabharata* and the *Ramayana*. For example, the story of Rama and Sita – the abduction of Sita by the cruel demon-king Ravana, the eventual defeat of Ravana and the establishment of the purity of Sita find repeated expression in Indian cinema. An early example is *Lanka Dahan* (Lanka Aflame, 1933). Secondly, there are films that deal with the lives and futures of religious saints. Thirdly, there are many films that deploy religious concepts and images as a way of investing the stories with greater significance. Fourthly, there are films that portray different religious cults. Fifthly, we find works of Indian cinema that seek to critique various religious institutions, practices and religiosities.

Among films depicting the lives and fortunes of saints is the already mentioned *Sant Tukaram*, made in 1936. The seventeenth century Maharashtra saint Tukaram willingly accepts the sufferings and atrocities heaped upon him by his oppressor, the Brahmin Salamalo, who falsely claims to be the true author of Tukaram's songs. In the end he is vindicated and triumphant. This film struck a chord with those who were turning away from the dominance of Sanskrit towards the vernaculars and the domination of the Brahmin caste.

Sant Tulsidas, made in 1939, is another. Tulsidas is well-known as the author who rewrote the original *Valmiki Ramayana*. To the utter dismay of his teacher, the poet spends his time with his beloved, Ratnavali. However, suddenly, and happily for everyone concerned, Tulsidas discovers his life's vocation during a storm. He becomes an ascetic and settles down in Benares to work on his translation. There has even been a film about a female saint, Sakhu. *Sant Sakhu*, made in 1945, recounts the life of a devoutly religious woman. She is married and is subjected to humiliations and hardships by her in-laws, until a series of miracles makes people realise that she is a saint.

Films dealing with the life of saints still continue to be made – *Adi Shankaracharya* (1983) by G.V Iyer is particularly interesting. The first film made in Sanskrit, it is set in Kerala in the eighth century and tells the story of Shankara, the best known Advaita Vedanta philosopher. Over three hundred Sanskrit texts are attributed to him. The film opens with Shankara as a boy, living in a village and being introduced to the Brahmanical rituals. After the death of his father, the boy is drawn towards philosophy, which he sees as a way of coming to grips with the mysteries of life. He leads the life of a mendicant and spends his time studying religious texts. He has little interest in marriage and leads 'a household life'. He tells his mother that he would remain a devoted son while leading the life of a mendicant scholar. His teacher entrusts him with the task of writing new commentaries to ancient religious texts at which he excels. He becomes an ascetic and travels to the Himalayas. By now he has a reputation as a man of learning. The film shows how by the age of thirty-two he succeeds in transcending all early illusions and becoming one with the Ultimate. Iyer made two other saint films, one about Madhavacharya (1986) and one about Shri Ramanujacharya (1989).

G.V Iyer's latest film is a cinematic representation of the *Bhagavad Gita* (1992). Asked why he chose this text for cinematic presentation, Iyer explained: 'The Gita is not just about the war, about Krishna talking to Arjun. It deals with the evolution of man and the teachings and the laws which were bestowed upon him, informing him about all the characteristics which are found in man. And how he has to conquer evil and reach the goal of self-realisation'. Clearly, he sees it as a text with a universally valid message.

Some of these 'saint' films have had a profound influence on the thought and imagination of a good many people. For example the film *Jai Santoshi Ma*, made in 1975 by Sharma, was instrumental in transforming a little-known goddess into a popular icon. She attained a wide acceptance among modern working class women toiling in the cities. Satyavati is the foremost disciple of the goddess Santoshi on earth. When Satyavati marries Birju, the wives of the three deities Brahma, Vishnu and Shiva become terribly jealous and create a series of problems and crises to test her faith and devotion. She emerges triumphantly from these tests and with her faith shining as ever, so she is admitted to the godly pantheon. Films dealing with the lives of saints deserve careful study as we pursue the interrelationships between religion and cinema in India.

Religious Symbolism in Film

The third category of religious films includes all those in which religious symbols, concepts and images play a key role in framing the narrative and investing it with meaning. As we look back on the evolution of Indian poetry, drama, sculpture, painting and so on, we see that religious concepts and images have been at the heart of the communicated experience. Even in films with no overt connection to religion in terms of plot or character, the imprint of religious ideas and images can be seen. Take an example from the work of popular film director Raj Kapoor – who cannot be described as a maker of religious films. He was primarily interested in producing popular romantic musicals that were secular in outlook but he nonetheless uses religious concepts to structure the narrative and give it a clearer focus. His film *Satyam Shivam Sundaram* made in 1978, focuses on the virtues of love, truth and beauty, the transforming power of love and its capacity to illuminate truth and genuine beauty. Like his other films, this one deals with romantic love through song and dance, but it consciously makes use of religious ideas to enhance the story.

The film *The Ritual* (1977) by Girish Kasaravalli provides another example. It has as its structuring device a Brahmanic ritual called 'ghata shradhda' through which Brahmin widows were excommunicated. The film relates how Yamuna, the young widowed daughter of a Brahmin scholar, is seduced by a school teacher and made pregnant. The close-knit Brahmin community is outraged and the father of Yamuna decides to perform the ritual 'ghata shradhdha' himself. Her head shaved, she is abandoned by the community. To be cast into widowhood is tantamount to falling from divine grace. To enjoy life as a widow is a sinful act which is irredeemable. Accordingly, anyone guilty of such acts is excommunicated through this ritual, which simulates the rituals of death on a living person. Indian cinema has produced many such films that are not religious but in which religious concepts are a way of organising the narrative.

Religious Cults and Institutions

A fourth category are the films that deal with specific religious cults, such as *Jai Santoshi Ma* (Santoshi Ma be praised!) or *Ishanou* (The Chosen One, 1990). The latter, made by Sharma, depicts the Meitei cult prevalent in Manipuri in India, inciting female adherents to join it by certain mystical powers that send them signals they cannot ignore. *Ishanou* is about a family that lives peacefully and happily in the Manipuri valley under the protection and care of an old woman. All of a sudden, the young wife Tampha becomes possessed by the deity Maibi and she leaves her home to be an active participant in the Maibi sect. The film contains exotic dances and rituals that illustrate for us the power of this religious cult.

Finally, films have, from the start, provided critiques of religious institutions, practices and understandings. Some have sought to point out the inequities of untouchability from the perspective of an enlightened humanism. More recently Satyajit Ray's *Devi* (Goddess, 1960) is notable and is discussed here in the section on women in Indian popular cinema. *Samskara* (Funeral Rites, 1970), also discussed in this book, reveals the dilemmas created by adhering too closely and rigidly to religious traditions. Questions of orthodoxy in religion are pitted against the changing social circumstances in a way that raises questions about the role of religious traditions in society.

Buddhist and Sikh Themes

The five categories discussed here relate to Hinduism, but a few films have been made in India that deal with other religions. *Angulimal* (1960) directed by Bhatt, is based on a well-known Buddhist story. Angulimal is a ruthless robber. He is called Angulimal because he wears a garland of human fingers cut from his victims' hands. He engages in bloody and cruel rituals in order to acquire divine powers. He encounters Buddha and sees the futility of his actions, repents for his past misdeeds and decides to follow the compassionate teachings of the Buddha. Here we find the confrontation of forces of light and darkness, creativity and destruction within a Buddhist philosophy.

Quoting extensively from the venerated Sikh text, the Granth Sahib, *Naanak Nam Jahaz Hai* (1969) explores aspects of a Sikh religious experience and seeks to capture the teachings of Guru Nanak. It narrates the story of Gurumukh Singh and his son Gurumeet. Gurumukh treats his partner Prem Singh as a younger brother until a business dispute ends their friendship. Prem Singh's wife wants her son Gurumeet to marry her niece Channi. During an argument she accidentally blinds him. Channi, the blind Gurumeet, and the repentant wife of Prem Singh set out on a pilgrimage of atonement, visiting all the Sikh shrines. Their troubled relationships are ultimately resolved at the famous Golden Temple in Amritsar. There, in response to Channi's prayers, a miracle takes place and Gurumeet's eyesight is restored.

Morality and Modernism

The relationship between religion and cinema in India can usefully be studied at another level also. Most of the films belong to the popular tradition of filmmaking and can be described as morality plays, where the forces of good and bad vie for supremacy. Plots are simple and little effort is made to portray complex human characters. In the contest between justice and injustice, light and darkness, wisdom and ignorance, the forces of justice, light and wisdom win out. What is interesting is that the movie-going public responds to them in the language and vocabulary of religious experiences, as Dissanayake and Sahai (1992) found when they interviewed hundreds of people in and around Delhi about such an extremely popular film as *Sholay*. People used expressions like 'It's all a matter of fate', 'God's will prevails in the end', 'The world was created with a purpose, and goodness has to triumph', 'What we see here is the action of karma', 'If you are devoted to God, no harm will come to you', 'One has to know one's dharma' and so on. The majority of film-goers in India look for morals in films and the power of God to set right injustice. The language in which they express these wishes is coloured by religious sentiments and religious convictions and merits closer study here.

India, like most other countries, is caught up in the process of modernisation. Some parts of the country are modernising at a faster pace than the others, but no region is unaffected. What this means is that questions of rationality, secularism, individuality, science and technology are foregrounded as never before. As a consequence one sees in modern Indian films – certainly those in the artistic tradition, but increasingly in popular films also – a conflict between religious values and modernising values. Some present this conflict as one between Westernisation and tradition – mistakenly. The real contest is between religious values and secular values, as films associated with the

New Indian Cinema demonstrate. So when we explore the topic of religion and cinema in India we need to pay close attention to this ongoing, and ever-increasing, contest between religious and secular values.

In modern Indian films, as opposed to many of the earlier films, one sees the emergence of a new kind of self as embodied in the character of the protagonist. This is certainly true of artistic films, but even in certain popular films such as Mani Rathnam's *Bombay* (1994), we can see this. Through the character of the journalist Shekhar, we see emerging a self which is secular, modern, suspicious of undue veneration of the past and desirous of bringing about ethnic and religious tolerance. A kind of liberal humanism pervades the outlook of these new heroes. We need to examine the nature and significance of such new thinking against the backdrop of religious belief in India to understand not only Indian cinema and its evolution but also some important aspects of Indian society and culture. Many cultural critics see this shift as significant in light of the fierce conflicts between religious groups which seem to tear apart the Indian social fabric.

In addition to the different and complex ways in which religious thought finds expression in Indian cinema and the contradictory pulls of religious and secular values in more recent films, gifted Indian filmmakers display cinematic sensibility to religious sentiments and symbols. G.Aravindan's *Chidambaram* (1985) is representative. Set on a commercial farm, the characters are not securely anchored to a solid and stable social order deriving sustenance from tradition, but are uprooted and transplanted into an artificial setting where they have to cultivate their individual selves.

Chidambaram deals with the complex relationships among four characters. Shankaran is an office superintendent on a farm located on the border of Kerala and Tamil Nadu. Jacob is a field supervisor, deeply conscious of his duties as well as the authority invested in him. Although their friendship is close, they are very different characters. Shankaran, who lives by himself, is well-liked by his subordinates. Jacob is pragmatic and proud, conscious of social hierarchy and he is not unduly perturbed by questions of morality and ethics. Muniyandi, who works as a labourer on this farm, is meek, submissive and deeply religious. He goes back to the village to get married and Shankaran, who is an amateur photographer, attends the wedding to take pictures. Shivagami, Muniyandi's wife, comes to live on the farm. She, like the rest of the characters in this film, is uprooted from her village environment and compelled to live in the artificial setting of the farm. At first she is totally overwhelmed by the strangeness, lushness and beauty of her new environment. The film shows beautifully, through carefully framed and vivid images, how she adjusts and comes to terms with her new surroundings. Shankaran becomes friendly with Shivagami, finding her extraordinarily gentle and attractive.

One day, Jacob comments in jest on Shankaran's interest in Shivagami, upsetting Shankaran, who hits him. Later he questions himself regarding his strange and inexplicable behaviour. Meanwhile, Jacob is trying hard to find employment for Shivagami on the farm. Muniyandi disapproves of the idea, but Shivagami is bored with doing nothing and eager to find work on the farm. Jacob finds her a job but Muniyandi, suspicious of Jacob's motives, turns down the offer. Jacob, annoyed and insulted, orders Muniyandi to work on the night shift. Muniyandi, overcome by growing suspicion, listens carefully to every sound as he works. One night, he hears a motorcycle making its way towards the house. In great anxiety, he rushes to the house and sees the shadow of a man slipping out of the back door. To his utter astonishment, it is not Jacob, as he had suspected, but his trusted supervisor Shankaran.

Early next morning, Muniyandi is found to have committed suicide. Shattered by this unexpected turn of events, Shankaran flees the farm and his life is transformed by the implacable power of guilt. He becomes an alcoholic, living a rootless existence in an artificial environment without the support of a stable community that he would find in a typical village and with no one to turn to. Shankaran wanders aimlessly; the doctor who treats him suggests that he immerses himself in religious texts and goes on holiday to places of religious significance. Shankaran starts to wander again and ends up at the famous Chidambaram temple. After visiting it, he pauses to put on his shoes and pay the haggard-looking woman who watches over them at the entrance. As she lifts up her face, Shankaran at once recognises Shivagami. He notes a deep scar on her face, probably indicating that Muniyandi beat her before he took his own life. Clearly, Shankaran has come to the end of his journey.

Chidambaram is the famous Hindu temple in South India where Lord Shiva was supposed to have been transformed into the famed cosmic dancer who enables human beings to free themselves from their earthiness and experience supramundane reality. The marvellously effective final sequence of the film takes place at the temple where, with imaginative camera work and accompanying thandava music, the earthly and supramundane levels of the film meet in exquisite union.

Aravindan, who has always been interested in exploring modes of religious and mythic consciousness in his films, is here introducing a metaphysical dimension. We have discussed this film at some length because it illustrates how even in films that do not deal with religious subjects or experiences, a religious sensibility operating on the creativity of the director can have intriguing results. There are many Indian films that manifest this tendency.

The emergence of a pronounced secular self in modern Indian society and cinema that is responding to the forces of modernisation, does not mean that religion has been eliminated from contemporary society. On the contrary, it has become an increasingly vital force. The rise of Hindu nationalism in India, like the rise of Muslim, Jewish or Christian fundamentalisms in other parts of the world, has taken most scholars by surprise. Why was the signi-ficant role that religion would assume in public life in most societies not pre-dicted? Was a simple antagonism between religion and modernity posited, with insufficient attention paid to the complex and multi-faceted ways in which they interact? Was the notion of modernity too simplistic to become a useful analytical tool in understanding the interplay of religion and society? These and similar questions are being heard today. What the latest writings on the subject seem to suggest is that religion did not disappear under the onslaught of modernisation; it merely relocated itself.

Daniel Bell explains the place of religion in modern society in terms of two separate causal chains: secularisation and profanation. He saw secularisation as the disengagement of religion from the public sphere and political life and religion as retreating into a private world. However, in the contemporary world, the exact opposite seems to have taken place. Religion is at the centre of the public sphere and political life. Many thoughtful filmmakers in India, as elsewhere, are beginning to question the received wisdoms about religion and society. In addition, we are seeing the increasing commodification of religious institutions and practices. Buying and selling mystical powers associated with religion is on the rise. A link between religion and profit-making is not new, but it has become far more widespread and international in outlook. Instant gurus, quacks, and charlatans give religion a bad name. All this does not go unnoticed by the more independent-minded filmmakers.

This broad review of religion in Indian cinema has indicated the valuable insights it affords into Indian society and Indian cinema. A study of a religion is also a study of the culture in which that religion flourishes. In the case of Islam, for example, although the central teachings may be universal, the ways in which they find cultural articulation differ according to the culture in which they are rooted, so Islam in India is not identical to Islam in Saudi Arabia or Iraq or Indonesia. The relationship between religion and society is evolving in India just as much as the representation of religion in cinema is evolving.

The Influence of the Cinema in the South of India

Although Bombay is usually considered the capital of the Indian film world, 'the film industry in the South, centred in Madras, is the largest in India in terms of the number of studios, capital investment, gross income and in the number of people engaged in the industry' (Hardgrave, 1975).

The glitter and excitement associated with Bombay is replaced in Madras by intense feeling for linguistic identity together with the promotion of the Dravidian Tamil heritage and this has led to cinema being used for political propaganda. In 1944, Annadurai founded the Dravida Munnetra Kazhagam (DMK) which eventually led to the downfall of the Congress Party in Madras and the election of Annadurai as the first DMK Chief Minister of Tamil Nadu.

However, it was the spectacular rise of M.G. Ramchandran (MGR), N.T.Rama Rao (NTR) and Jayalalitha and the 'divine' powers attributed to them by their fans which turned them into starry politicians. In his films, MGR saw himself as the 'protector' of the common man and he is convinced of the moral purpose of his films: 'My roles have been to show how a man should live and believe'. Mother tongue, motherland and motherhood were the stuff on which MGR's popularity was founded. 'Backed by a powerful party, aided by one million fan clubs spread all over the state, he became the Chief Minister of Tamil Nadu in the 1970s and stayed in power for ten years.' (Garga 1996:269). Garga gives an example of the emotional response that MGR could evoke 'when in 1987 during a critical illness, 22 people committed suicide in the hope that their deaths would somehow save their leader' (Garga 1996:269).

The same adulation is given to NTR and Jayalalitha. NTR played the mythological Gods, Rama and Krishna, in over 100 feature films and his fans deified him as the Omnipotent, the Omniscient and Omnipresent. Jayalalitha not only succeeded MGR as the Chief Minister, but was also an enormously influential actress. At the height of her acting career, she received huge numbers of letters from her fans, some requesting her to send her photo to cure illnesses. Her supporters have committed bizarre acts, prostrating themselves before her or 'rolling on the streets to show their devotion to her'. (Garga 1996:270). As Hardgrave (1975) rightly observes, star worship represents a cathartic identification: 'the world of the film star becomes a repository of displaced frustration. The star provides the avenue of escape from the tedium of everyday life, from the desperation of poverty'.

Ethnicity and Caste

In recent years the concept of ethnicity has gained intellectual respectability, particularly through the development of Cultural Studies. Issues of ethnicity, identity and the problem of minorities are crucially linked. Ethnicity is difficult to define precisely but an ethnic group can be described as a self-conscious collection of people united, or closely related, by characteristics acquired at birth (colour, for example) and/or by culturally shared experiences such as language, religion and caste.

Hindu-Muslim Conflict

When we talk about ethnicity and the problems of minorities in India, the conflict between Hindus and Muslims comes immediately to mind. After the partitioning of India in 1947, most Muslims settled in the newly formed state of Pakistan but today there are over one hundred million Muslims living in India. Periodically, open and often violent conflicts occur between Hindus and Muslims in India. A number of filmmakers have sought to focus on this issue in their work and three films that deal with the Hindu-Muslim conflict in India are now briefly discussed.

The first is by Hindu filmmaker M.S.Sathyu. *Garam Hava* (Hot Winds, 1975) narrativises the collective brutal violence against the Muslims during partition. To dramatise this violence on screen Sathyu has focused on the misfortunes and privations of a single family. Salim Mirza (superbly played by Balraj Sahni) is a shoe manufacturer whose family has lived in Agra for generations. With partition in 1947, Mirza, like thousands of other Muslims, was faced with the unpalatable choice of leaving India for the newly created state of Pakistan or stay and incurring the collective hostilities of the Hindu majority in India. His elder brother, Halim a shrewd politician, resolves to leave India, but Mirza will not. In his bones, he feels that India is his country and he wants to remain behind and continue with the family business. As Salim Mirza's daughter Amina is engaged to Halim's son Kazim, the situation becomes more complicated. The border between India and Pakistan is closed off, and Kazim is prohibited from coming back to meet his bride. He succeeds after much effort in crossing the border illegally and preparations are hastily made for the wedding, but the police show up and Kazim is apprehended.

The agonies and hardships resulting from the partitioning begin to affect Mirza's life. He loses his business, and his daughter commits suicide. The film conveys Mirza's miseries honestly and movingly, if a little sentimentally. At last after much agonising, he decides to accept the inevitable and leave India with his son. As they make their way to the railway station for their departure, they find themselves among a procession of protesters of diverse social, political, religious, ethnic affiliations. All of them belong to marginalised and disenfranchised groups. Mirza abandons his plans to leave the country and joins the protesters in the hope that their clamour will awaken the people to the mindless violence around them and make public opinion more enlightened.

In *Garam Hava* director Sathyu has highlighted the plight of Muslims in India with sympathy and understanding. A Hindu himself, he has sought to promote a keener appreciation of the difficulties and hardships encountered by minorities. The film reminds us that the nation of India is made up of diverse ethnic, linguistic, religious groups and that the rights of each of the group need to be protected. *Garam Hava* is a good example of how the camera helps us to share the humdrum daily living of 'ordinary' families: people make tea, the father reads a newspaper, the mother sews a dress and a young girl sits on a bed trying on bangles, while the bangle-seller woman sits on the floor. As we feel the web of relations holding members of the family together, we share their pain as this web disintegrates under the strain of partition. Khanna (1980) has provided a detailed reading of *Garam Hava*. One of his central points is that although the film 'fails to analyse the causes either of the partition or the sufferings undergone by individuals', it vividly depicts the daily lives in a Muslim household to people in India who have had only slight acquaintance with Muslims.

The second film that deals with the Hindu-Muslim conflict is Saeed Akhtar Mirza's *Salim Langde Pe Mat Ro* (Don't Cry for Salim the Lame, 1989). It centres on the life and fortunes of Salim, a young Muslim attempting to carve out an identity for himself in a hostile world. Salim is poor and leads a life of crime, his role models being racketeers and smugglers who have achieved material success by brazenly defying the law; his sought-after world pays little respect to moral values. He lives in a world of poverty, moral degradation, crime and violence. If Salim represents 'the self-destructive element among Muslim youth, his counterpoint is provided by Aslam, highly educated and idealistic, who can find no job other than that of a low-paid proof reader' (Garga 1996:257). Although Salim tries to embrace a more compassionate view of life, the operative logics of his social world would have none of it. In the midst of celebrations for his sister's wedding, Salim is knifed to death by a member of a rival gang.

In *Don't Cry for Salim the Lame*, the intention of the director is to focus attention on the Muslims in India, especially those living in the cities. The film has as its theme the question of belonging and unbelonging in modern India, and how the nation-state can marginalise the minorities in most unsatisfactory ways. The director has underlined the need to take very seriously the problems and hardships of the Muslim minority if gratuitous violence is to be avoided.

The third film dealing with this complicated and troubled relationship (and mentioned earlier) is by the Hindu filmmaker Mani Rathnam. It is more recent and it generated heated debate in India and even assassination attempts. *Bombay* (1994) deals with forbidden love, against the backdrop of Hindu-Muslim conflict. The story centres around the love between a Hindu journalist and a Muslim girl whose parents are implacably opposed to it. They run away to the city of Bombay and get married. They have two children and their parents begin to accept them. However, as things brighten up on the personal front, violence breaks out in Bombay as a consequence of the mounting tensions between Hindus and Muslims.

Mani Rathnam is careful not to favour either the Hindu or the Muslim point of view but, as was to be expected, the film was highly controversial and led to protests from both communities. In fact, *Bombay* encapsulates many of the issues regarding the cultural differences between Hindus and Muslims and their representation in films. It is time that the sectarian violence and the incidents which wrought havoc in Bombay in 1992/1993 were used in film as part of the narrative. The dichotomy between the village and the city (discussed earlier, particularly in our analysis of the films of the 1950s) is again emphasised but in a different light – inter-communal conflict in the village as against the city. Over the past 40 years, Indian popular cinema has almost always highlighted the Hindu hero; here, however, the character of the Hindu journalist is there for Mani Rathnam to argue for a more enlightened attitude towards the relationship between Hindus and Muslims. Mani Rathnam is following previous film directors in search of harmony among the communities and shows that there are no winners in the inhumanity of communal strife. The filmmaker, through the character of the Hindu journalist, pleads for rational thinking and a more enlightened attitude. These three films, in their different ways and from their distinctive vantage points, are among a number that have dealt with this issue.

The Parsis

Muslims are only one minority in India, The Parsis are another. Followers of prophet Zoroaster and descendants of Persian Zoroastrians, they immigrated to India in the eighth century to avoid religious persecution by the Muslims.

They are a commercially successful ethnic group who are known for their wealth as well as their beneficence and constitute an important subculture of India. Since establishing themselves in India as a distinct ethnic group they have contributed significantly to the commercial, scientific and artistic life of the country. *Pestonjee* (1987), directed by Vijaya Mehta, seeks to capture an aspect of the complex reality of the Parsis. The film deals with the culture, way of life and conventions that govern the social life of the influential Parsi community of India. The human drama captured in this film gains depth and definition from the dynamics of this subculture. The film presents the life of Piroj and his deep friendship with Pesi. Mehta has expanded on a short story by B.K.Karanjia in a way that allows her to probe the characters more comprehensively.

Pirojshau (Piroj) and Pestonjee (Pesi) are close friends and bachelors. Some-one suggested to Piroj that he marry Jeroo, a girl of romantic dreams. But characteristically Piroj cannot decide immediately and meanwhile, Pesi agrees to marry her. Once Pesi is a married man, the relationship between Piroj and Pesi undergoes certain changes. Piroj is transferred to the town of Bhusaval and the marital relationship between Pesi and Jeroo is subject to various strains. Piroj receives a letter from Pesi informing him that Jeroo is expecting a baby; filled with joy, Piroj resolves to visit them. On his arrival, he realises that things are not bright and happy as he had expected. Pesi had begun to have an affair and Piroj disapproves. Pesi resents his friend's desire to run his life. The two friends drift apart, vowing never to meet again.

Three years pass. Unexpectedly, Piroj receives a New Year card from Pesi, intimating that he misses Piroj greatly. Meanwhile, Piroj is transferred to Bombay and the two friends meet briefly and try, with little success, to revive their friendship. The following morning Pesi dies of a heart attack. Sum-marised in this fashion, *Pestonjee* may appear somewhat sentimental and there is certainly a strain of sentimentality in the film. But it is counter-balanced by the comic observations of the director and the humour generated by the dialogue as well as the acting. From our point of view, what is interesting about this film is the way the three main characters are securely situated in the Parsi sub-culture and how the customs, beliefs, rituals, values associated with the Parsis frame the entire experience.

The Theme of Ethnicity
Ethnicity figures in other interesting ways in Indian cinema. In popular films, ethnic stereotypes are sometimes presented for comic effect. Indeed, the link between Sanskrit drama and popular cinema continues through familiar and

sometimes well-paid comedians. According to Valicha (1988:73), a comic interlude has been traditionally regarded as an essential feature of every popular film. Each comedian specialises in a certain type of comic ability: Johnny Walker evoking a rustic element, Gope the witless fool, Mehmood an earthy and sensual humour. The comic characters are very often visually different from the heroes; for example, Mukri, who is short and slow witted.

Occasionally the need is stressed for ethnic harmony and authenticity. As Valicha (1988,75) put it: 'while the film in its totality perpetuates an apparently false world of artifice and luxury, the comic seems to break that overbearing illusion and pour out, in a bucolic and homely manner, affirmations of everyday life. It seems to give the film a ring of authenticity'. At other times, national unity is stressed with great sentimentality. For example in *Amar, Akbar, Anthony* (1977) which tells the story of a Hindu, a Muslim and a Christian, the joy of national unity and inter-ethnic harmony is celebrated.

Whether this is rhetoric or reality very often depends on the national and the international situation. For example, the fluctuating relationship between India and Pakistan over the Kashmir issue, the campaign to establish Khalistan and the rise of Hindu nationalism have dented the fabric of a multi-religious India. What happens to India will largely depend on how powerful Hindu nationalism becomes – for example, the influence of Bal Thackaray's Shiv Shena in Maharastra. And this in turn will have serious consequences on the Indian cinema, where inter-ethnic harmony has always been celebrated.

The Asian Diaspora
Different notions of ethnicity emerge when we consider ethnic minorities settled abroad. For example, until recently the Asian perspective in British film culture has generally been excluded. There have been quite a number of Asian film-makers working in Britain (e.g. Waris Hussain, Jamil Dehlavi, Ismail Merchant) who did not present the Asian experience. It could even be argued that they confirmed the West's fascination with the Orient, the exotic, in films such as *Gandhi, A Passage to India, Heat and Dust, Jewel in the Crown*, in which the nostalgia of the 'Raj' is reworked. In his insightful article 'Locating the Asian Experience', Perminder Dhillon-Kashyap (1988) comments:

> These nostalgic tales of the 'Raj' reiterate and intensify the same colonial images – of the 'other', the 'darkie', the 'alien' – which were created and used to justify colonialism, while making a pretence of questioning the morality of imperialism. Thus beguiling the audience, implicit cultural discriminations are presented as 'truths'. Colonial

atrocities by the British are then presented as deeds of extreme personalities (policeman Merrick in the *Jewel in the Crown* and Colonel Dyer in *Gandhi*).

Since the 1980s, however, there have been some Asian screenwriters and directors who have made an impact on the big and small screens. Hanif Kureishi's *My Beautiful Laundrette* (1985) received wide acclaim although his *Sammy and Rosie Get Laid* (1987) was less successful. Nair's *Salaam Bombay* (1988) is more of a documentary of dispossessed youth living on their wits in an uncaring city.

Nair's *Mississippi Masala* (1991) created a stir among the Asians because of its love affair between the Asian, Sarita Choudhury and the 'black' American, Denzel Washington. However, it was *Bhaji on the Beach* (1993) which caught the imagination of Asians in Britain. This is a 'tale of two generations of Asian women on a day trip to Blackpool and includes a Punjabi version of Summer Holiday' (*The Guardian* 15/11/96 p.5). The significant contribution of diasporic Indian filmmakers is discussed in chapter 7.

Caste

Ethnicity is one social division in India: another is caste where the division is found within the Hindu social order. No other institution in India has so exercised the imagination of foreigners as the caste system. It is highly complex, so has been frequently misinterpreted. The word 'caste' derives from the Portuguese word *casta* meaning colour – and colour forms an important part of the Indian caste system. Caste is basically a system of social classification, a mechanism by which people are grouped into traditionally sanctioned categories. All categorisations are based on certain accepted criteria. The concepts of purity and pollution are central to the Indian caste system. Behind it lies a complex world of classification – of things, actions and thoughts in terms of their relative purity and impurity and their relative power to pollute. Contact, either directly or obliquely, with things that are deemed impure results in pollution and has to be removed through various acts of ritual purification. This caste classification system has separated people in terms of professional activities – priests, landowners, merchants, cultivators, artisans, menials and so on.

The caste system originated with the Indo-European nomadic tribes generally known as Aryans, who made their way to India over thirty thousand years ago. These tribes originally came as pastoral raiders, but later merged with the indigenous population and settled down in India. Historians tell us that they came in distinct waves, the earliest arriving in India in about 1300 BC. Before long many of the non-Aryan tribes living in the country were Aryanized. The Aryan word for the native was 'dasa', which literally means slave, and this class was incorporated into the newly established Aryan social order called 'sudras' and with this amalgamation, a new social hierarchy emerged. Initially, there were four classes: Brahmin (priest), Kshatriya (warrior), Vaishya (trader) and Sudra (cultivator). This four-fold division gave rise to the elaborate caste system. Below the Sudras are the untouchables, often referred to as the 'Scheduled Castes'. Their extremely degraded status derived from their performing certain menial and dirty tasks. In recent years, many call themselves *dalits* (oppressed) and have revolted against their status.

Caste is an important institution in Indian society, which the rapid modernisation of Indian society has invested with much tension. Caste

e divisions have formed the backdrop of many Indian films, both popular and
h artistic, from the very beginning. *Achut Kanya* (1936) and *Sujata* (1959) for
example, sought to alert public opinion about the ill-effects of caste
distinctions. Bimal Roy's *Sujata* (1959) deals with the issue of caste in relation to romantic love and individual desire. Sujata is an untouchable. As an
infant, she is taken care of by an engineer and his wife of the Brahmin caste.
This arrangement is intended to be only temporary and it is assumed that
suitable arrangements would be made. However, no home is found for her,
and the family grows fond of her and raises her as a daughter. A marriage is
arranged for their real daughter, Rama with Adhir, whose family becomes
concerned that an untouchable girl is living with Rama's family. However,
they resolve that the marriage should go ahead as planned and that Sujata
should be married off to a suitable person. They insist that Sujata should not
be present at Rama and Adhir's wedding. However, things do not work out as
they anticipate. Adhir falls in love with Sujata and wants to marry her instead

of Rama. Films like *Achut Kanya* and *Sujata* served to focus attention on how the caste system operates in India.

At times, the theme of caste is treated in terms not of inter-caste interactions but of the dynamics within one caste group. One example is *Samskara* (Funeral Rites, 1970), based on the widely discussed novel by U.R. Ananthamurthy. It deals with the inner workings of the close-knit community of Madhava Brahmins. One of the group is Naranappa, always a heretic who defied the accepted norms of behaviour. Having broken all the sacred codes of the Brahmins by eating meat, drinking, and keeping a mistress of low caste, Naranappa dies of plague. His death presents the Brahmins of this group with a problem: who will perform the final funeral rites for him? As long as the defiled body of Naranappa lies in his home, it is not possible for his family members or other Brahmins to eat or even have a drink of water. Any Brahmin who touched the body of Naranappa would be defiled. The film explores this predicament.

The question of caste and its ramifications finds expression not only in popular cinema but also in artistic films, for example, Satyajit Ray's *Sadgati* (*Deliverance*), made for television in 1981. Based on a short story by the celebrated Hindi writer Premchand, the film explores how the discourse of caste intersects with other important social institutions and practices. Pandit Ghashiram is a powerful Brahmin priest who lives in a small village and performs sacrificial ceremonies and advises the villagers about auspicious and inauspicious times. In this village lives a poor untouchable by the name of Dukhi. His daughter is about to get married, and he wants Pandit Ghashiram to help him select an auspicious date for his daughter's wedding. Pandit Ghashiram promises to help him and Dukhi agrees to do manual labour for him in return. Dukhi is asked to chop an old trunk of a tree into small pieces with an axe. The wood is hard and he fails to cut the tree trunk. He is exhausted and longs to smoke his clay pipe. As he has no matches to light, he goes into Pandit Ghashiram's house to ask the wife of Pandit Ghashiram for some charcoal. She is outraged; she cannot believe that an untouchable dare enter her house. Dukhi goes back and starts to chop down the tree. He collapses and dies and, in this predominantly Brahmin village, the corpse of an untouchable lying there becomes a public nuisance.

Satyajit Ray portrays these events in a way that brings out the meaning of duty and caste system as well as questions of exploitation, tradition, modernity, and private and public morality. These same issues are explored from a different angle in Ghosh's *Antarjali Yatra* (The Voyage Beyond, 1987). Although sati is the dramatic core of the film (see Rajadhyaksha and Willemen, 1994:443 for an outline of the plot), the close physical proximity between the 'untouchable' Baiju and the Brahmin's bride awakens the latter's sexuality. The setting is a cremation ground and Ghosh uses the camera to bring the scenes remarkably to life through light, space, motion and colour. At the same time, Ghosh delivers a powerful blow to tradition and the caste system.

In India's multi-racial, multi-religious society, social issues connected with ethnic conflicts and ethnic strife are inevitably explored by Indian film-makers. Hinduism is the predominant religion in India, and the Hindu religion sets great store by the caste system. As India, like all societies, is subject to modernisation, the caste system becomes challenged by notions of equality, citizenship and democratic participation. Many filmmakers sensitive to such issues find the caste system an important site in which to examine social issues vital to India.

CHAPTER 5

Women in Indian Cinema

The complex and fascinating relationship between women and cinema has a substantial literature and there is some interesting work on Third World feminism, which illuminates aspects of the representation of women in Indian films.

Here, we focus attention on two areas: the representation *of* women and the representation *by* women on screen. Both aspects are essential for understanding the interplay between women and cinema in India. It is useful to deal first with the representation of women in the popular and artistic cinema, referring to a number of illustrative examples.

The Representation of Women on the Screen

In traditional Indian society, there were definite and consensual norms of behaviour – that regulated the conduct of women – all of them handed down from the past. For example, the concept of woman as *Sita* is prevalent in Indian society as well as Indian films. *Sita*, immortalised in the *Ramayana*, is the ideal woman, the ideal wife; she is steadfastly loyal to her husband and obeys his wishes unquestioningly. The *Ramayana* says that a wife's god is her husband: he is her friend, her teacher. Her life is of less consequence than her husband's happiness. Over the years, Indian popular cinema had perpetuated this ideal of a wife's selfless devotion.

In traditional Indian society, the lives of women were severely circumscribed. Strict rules and regulations had to be followed. Women's roles were essentially as daughter (Beti), wife (Patni) and mother (Ma). According to the *Manusmriti*, which had a profound effect on shaping the morals of Indian society, a female should be subject in childhood to her father, in youth to her husband, and when her husband is dead, to her children. Women were given no kind of independence. *Manusmriti* is emphatic that a woman must not strive to separate herself from her father, her husband, her sons. She is told to be always cheerful, efficient in the management of household affairs, fastidious in cleaning utensils, careful with expenses. She is expected to be unwaveringly obedient to her husband, and after he is dead she must make every effort to honour his memory. These norms governed the lives of women in traditional India, and they find clear articulation in Indian cinema, especially in popular films.

Not that romantic love was prohibited for women. If that were the case, many popular Indian films would not have been made. Women were permitted to indulge in romantic love if it followed the *Radha-Krishna* model. In classical Indian texts, the love of *Radha* for *Krishna* is all-consuming, absolutely pure, and eternal and this is the kind of romantic love depicted in mainstream Indian films. Women who seek to live by the traditional norms find happiness, while those who dare to transgress them are punished and victimised, as a few representative examples will illustrate.

In *Do Anjane* (Two Strangers) made in the seventies, a woman who tries to defy the prescribed code of conduct is severely punished. This wife who wants to pursue a career as a classical Indian dancer is portrayed as self-centred and arrogant, causing her husband economic hardships and then leaving him. However, the husband she impoverished ultimately becomes rich and successful and highly esteemed by society, while she suffers all the indignities of a society that finds her a decadent woman.

Thodisi Bewafayi (1980) is another popular film with the same moral. The daughter (played by talented actress Shabana Azmi) of an indulgent father decides to marry the man with whom she is in love. Her husband loses his money and becomes poor. Instead of making use of her education, securing a job and improving the family fortunes, she resolves to go back to her father – but he too loses his job. She then goes to her brother's house, where her brother's wife begins to dislike her intensely. She ends up defeated, overwhelmed by misery and keen to go back to her husband.

However, there have always been films that challenge this treatment of women. For example, V. Shantaram's *Duniya Na Mane* (Uncompromising World, 1957), highly valued by Indian film historians, concerns an orphaned young woman who is tricked into marriage with an old man by her uncle who is greedy for money and who, with great strength of character, refuses to perform any of the wifely duties expected of her by society. The husband comes to realise the evils of his action as well as the injustices heaped upon women by society. In order to grant her the kind of freedom that she deserves, he takes his life.

Two roles that are of particular significance in Indian popular cinema are those of mother and wife, and there is a disparity between the representation of these two roles. It is a worldwide practice to think of one's country as one's 'motherland' but Indian reference to the mother is loaded with religious significance and the country is conflated with the mother goddess, Shakti (literally strength). The concept of the country as mother finds resonance in the national hymn *Vandemataran!* (Hail 'Mother (land)'), and the mother in Indian films is always revered as a vital force in society – as in *Mother India* (1957), which is in many ways the 'quintessential Indian film' (Thomas, 1989).

Yet although the wife is represented as a victim of social conventions and her individuality is severely limited, the word Shakti is used to describe her role as mother in Indian films. More appropriate to describe the wife may be the word Sati (extreme devotion to her husband). The Sati concept led to a considerable number of films in the 1920s and 1930s (e.g *Sati Parvati*, 1920; *Sati Anjani*, 1922; *Sati Ansuya*, 1933; *Sati Seeta*, 1924; *Sati Savitri*, 1927) and, although it is no longer fashionable, its effect was to portray women as stereotypical, unidimensional creatures with no personal ambitions of their own.

Nevertheless, this ideal wife *must* be sexually pure and the epitome of sexual fidelity. As Richards (1995) observes, the Hindi film upholds the 'traditional patriarchal views of society which, fearful of female sexuality, demands of the woman a subjugation of her desires' (p3). Consistent with the cultural norms pertaining to the status of women in Indian society, the honour of the family (Izzat) is closely linked to female behaviour. The need to preserve honour is expressed through 'elaborate, codified behaviour patterns that require the woman to remain secluded, confined to the domestic domain and dependent on the husband.'

The opposite of the wife is the vamp, normally a decadent modern woman, generally with a name like Rosie or Mary. She flouts tradition and seeks to imitate western women. She drinks, smokes, visits night clubs and is quick to fall in and out of love. She is portrayed as a morally degraded person and has come to be associated with everything that is unwholesome about the west. And she is almost always punished for her unacceptable behaviour. There is an interesting contradiction here. Indian cinema is a product of cultural modernity and it has accelerated the process of modernity in India as few other media have. Yet the woman who chooses to identify herself with modernity is almost always portrayed as decadent and punished for it.

Another frequent representation of womanhood in mainstream Indian cinema is the courtesan. The courtesan is commonly found in classical art and literature, ministering to the physical and emotional needs of men. The courtesan in Indian films is represented as existing outside the normal domain of domesticity and she is deeply attracted to the protagonist of the film, although usually he does not fall in love with her. She provides him with comfort, care, physical happiness and then, when he has adequately recovered from the miseries he has had to contend with and goes back to his sanctioned life, she pines for him. This theme, which was clearly established in such films as *Devdas* (1935), has continued to affect audiences. There have been films that contravene this pattern, such as *Chetna,* made in 1970 which tells the story of a young man who falls in love with a beautiful girl only to discover that she is a prostitute but is so attracted to her that he marries her.

Indian popular films are largely romantic musicals, and romance plays a significant role. The female protagonist is beautiful and the camera always makes a point of capturing her beauty in sensual detail. She becomes an object of male desire just as in American and European films. But the ways in which the female form is displayed in Indian popular films are culture-specific.

Kissing is a sensitive issue. In 'The State and Culture: Hindi cinema on the Passive Revolution' Prasad (1994) offers an illuminating discussion on the theme of kissing. According to Prasad, the prohibition of kissing scenes was based on an unwritten rule; the written rules 'prohibited excessively pas-sionate love scenes', 'indelicate sexual situations' and 'scenes suggestive of immorality', all of which were derived from the British code of Censorship applied in Britain as well as (with modification) in British India' (ibid, p.173). Public kissing is associated with western life, so is alien to Indian culture. But the paradox is that the restrictions have never been applied in the censorship of foreign films. Furthermore, while the majority of the Indian audience as well as many notable film personalities would appear to favour the ban on scenes of kissing in Indian films, the vulgarity in the depiction of sexual activity in Indian films is transparent and this is difficult to reconcile with the ban on scenes of kissing.

How then is sexuality conveyed? The Indian cinema excels in the matter of disguised acts of sexual excitement by operating on the basis that the female form nude is less exciting than veiled. Richards (1995) has identified strategies used to display the female form and female sexual desire:

(a) **Tribal Dress** It is in the song and cabaret dance numbers that 'tribal costumes are used for the exposure of vast expanses of the body, in particular the pelvic region'. Richards (1995:5) notes that the short skirts, brief blouses and veil-less upper torso allow for maximum female exposure in Hindi films, that will not invite opprobrium from the nation's moral authorities.

(b) **Dream sequences/wet saris** A second device is the 'wet sari dance' which is, according to Richards (1995): 'legitimised by a sudden, torrential downpour that soaks the woman's flimsy sari, and allows for a very provocative and sexually tantalising exposure of the female body'. Allied to this device is the strategy of dream sequences. These dream sequences provide the freedom to indulge in the exploration of forbidden pleasures which include the display of the female body as well as the expression of sexual desire.

In *Deewana* (Madly in Love, 1967), Rishi Kapoor and Divyabharati fall in love and marry. Halfway through the film Rishi Kapoor is killed. When Shahrukh Khan sees his widow, he immediately falls in love with her. But as she is a grieving widow, she ignores his attentions. Dressed in white, her only activity is a daily visit to the temple. But Shahrukh Khan refuses to be discouraged by this and lying in bed, he drifts into a reverie and, in a dream sequence constructed around a song and dance number, he frolics with Divjabharati, now transformed into a modern, energetic woman.

(c) **Behind the Bush** The song and dance sequences often give rise to another strategy which allows the dancing couple to retreat behind a bush or a tree and after a pause the heroine emerges into the frame wiping her lips. Prasad (1994:177-178) presents this as 'a public confirmation of a private act which has cultural associations with a certain feudal practice of communal eroticism that consists of the display of the marks of sexual initiation on the female body'. Such erotic display of the female body in the popular cinema can be explained by the ideology of the public sphere. 'The female body as spectacle is a public representation, a putting before the public of an erotic imagery that does not violate the code that prohibits the representation of the private'. This is permissible because the song and dance sequences are conventionally coded as contracted voyeurism. (Kissing, on the other hand, belongs to the realm of the private.)

Voyeurism

Mulvey (1975) notes how through its codes and conventions, the cinema constructs the way in which women are to be looked at – scopophilia – pleasure in viewing. As holder of the gaze, the spectator is positioned voyeuristically, desiring to look, with all that that connotes in terms of fetishism. This is clearly illustrated in *Dastak* (The Knock, 1970) which achieved notoriety for a single shot lasting just a couple of seconds, in which Rehana Sultan appears in the nude. The film tells the story of a young Muslim couple Hamid and Salma, who move into an apartment in Bombay unaware that its previous tenant was a *tawaif* (an entertainer/prostitute). Her customers, not knowing that she has moved, come and knock on the door and disturb the young couple. The young people living in an apartment opposite look into the apartment and watch Salma (the young wife) as she bathes and dresses. But there is more to it. When her husband Hamid goes away to work, Salma is alone and, unaware that she is being watched by the men across the street, enacts her fantasies. 'The film hovers between the two spaces in which woman's sexuality is distributed: the home and the brothel.' In the former, woman's sexuality is reduced to its reproductive functions; in the latter, it is pure and explicit sexuality, available to all.

In the artistic cinema, directors associated with the New Cinema sought to present a very different image of women – women not as objects of male desire, but as products of diverse social formations and seeking to transcend their sordid circumstances. These directors are interested in capturing the plight of women as they are caught in the contradictory pulls of tradition and modernity, past and present, and individuality and community. Satyajit Ray's *Mahanagar* (Metropolis) is a good example. Made in 1963, it seeks to explore the influence of urbanisation on the character and behaviour patterns of a woman who, like many women in India and elsewhere, is increasingly subject to the forces of urbanisation. *Mahanagar* relates the problems and privations of Arati and her husband Subrata, who live in Calcutta. Subrata works as an accountant in a bank but his income is insufficient to meet his family obligations, so he suggests that Arati should look for employment too. At first Arati dislikes the idea but she later consents to become a salesgirl. Subrata's father, a traditionalist, is appalled by this idea, despite Subrata's attempts to convince him that times have changed. With the landing of a job, a whole new world opens up before Arati. She finds the job interesting and the people with whom she works likeable. Her boss, Mukherjee, grows to love her. Arati's father-in-law, however, steadfastly refuses to accept the money she brings home.

Arati's behaviour and outlook begin to change. The urban environment to which she is exposed is clearly having a profound impact on the way she thinks, feels and acts. She has entered the modern world. This change arouses a measure of anxiety in her husband, and through the help of an influential friend, he succeeds in securing a second job which he does after bank hours. He persuades Arati that, now that he has a second job she need no longer work. Next day, Arati goes to the office with her letter of resignation. Meanwhile, Subrata has lost his job and tries to prevent his wife from quitting hers, but events that follow leave her no option but to hand in her resignation.

In films like these we find an attempt to capture the complexities of modern life and their impact on women. Questions of rights and obligations, duties and privileges, independence and respect for authority, and other related issues influencing the life of women in India are being increasingly explored through cinema by directors associated with the New Indian Cinema.

The Representation of Women by Women Film Makers/Directors

Next, we need to examine the work of female directors, only recently emerging, and how they seek to portray the lives and experiences of women. During the last three decades a number of talented women film directors have appeared on the Indian cinema scene. Among them, Prema Karanth, Aparna Sen, Vijaya Mehta, Sai Paranjpye, Parvati Ghosh, Vijaya Nirmala, Suprabha Debi, Bhanumathi and Kalpana Lajmi deserve special mention. A few of the films made by female directors in India are now discussed in light of the themes and issues that these works explore. Almost all these directors have shown a great interest in examining the experiences, problems and hardships encountered by women, from the viewpoint of women. It has been argued by some women film critics that even the most liberal-minded and well-meaning of male film directors in India still display some residual patriarchal leanings. So it is interesting to examine how women filmmakers in India are seeking to capture cinematically the experiences of women as they explore the complex terrain of modern life.

Accordingly we have selected four women film directors – Prema Karanth, Vijaya Mehta, Aparna Sen and Kalpana Lajmi. They expose some of the tensions and contradictory pressures connected with the representation of female subjectivity in the context of the family in Indian cinema. Prema Karanth, a gifted director from Karnataka, was art director of two films, *Hamsa Geethe* (1975) and *Kudre Motte* (1977). However, the film that we wish to discuss is her *Phaniyamma* (Aunt Phani, 1982).

Phaniyamma

Based on a novel by M.K.Indira, the film explores the question of female identity in an essentially male-dominated society through the life of a woman over a seventy-year period, against the background of Brahmin orthodoxy. Phani is a good-natured little girl who helps with the various household chores of the older women while her brother attends the local school. At the age of nine, as custom would have it, her horoscope is meticulously studied and compared with that of one of her equally young relatives. As the horoscopes match admirably, the elders resolve to arrange a marriage. Phani and her child husband go through the marriage ceremony, the camera beautifully catching their bewilderment and boredom. After the marriage ceremonies are over, Phani's husband goes back to his village, and she goes to live with her uncle until she reaches puberty.

Unfortunately, this carefully mapped-out scenario goes sour when Phani's little husband dies from a snake bite, and she is left a widow while still a child. Widowhood entails various humiliations and derogations. Her wedding chain (mangalsutra) is taken away; her attractive bangles are broken; the red mark on her forehead is wiped away. When she reaches puberty, her head is shaved in accordance with traditional custom. From then she is obliged to go about bald-headed, dressed in a white sari to signify her widowed state and to make herself as unattractive as possible to the opposite sex. Interestingly, as a consequence of the activities of the social reformers, the Hindu Widow's Remarriage Act and the Child Marriage Restraint Act had by then entered the statute books.

Cut off from her usual social activities, Phani endures her suffering in silence, not quite understanding the reasons for her miserable existence. As she matures, she decides to rise above the sterility of her life and invest it with meaning by helping others in society. As time passes, the unfortunate and bewildered child widow becomes the caring and compassionate Aunt Phani, a highly esteemed and much loved woman in the village who goes about helping others. She also begins to question and challenge some of the customs people have unthinkingly upheld. She helps with the complicated birth to a woman who belongs to the untouchable class. She pours scorn on the hypocrisy of a man who sleeps with an untouchable woman and ritually purifies himself the following morning. A young woman who is treated harshly by her husband for her inability to bear children is persuaded by Phani to take the extraordinarily daring step of leaving him.

Phani's growth into emotional maturity and self-confidence is vividly brought to life in one episode. Dakshyani, a sixteen year-old widow, defiantly

84

refuses to have her head shaved as dictated by custom or to subject herself to other humiliations connected with widowhood. Her mother-in-law and other villagers are outraged by her defiance. Phani is the only person who is bold enough to side with Dakshyani; she points out that as times have changed, people need to relinquish outdated customs and obsolete ways of thinking and adopt more modern and enlightened attitudes. Dakshyani succeeds in holding her ground; she keeps her long hair and wears bright-coloured clothes. Eight months later she becomes pregnant and announces that she is planning to marry the father of the child, her brother-in-law. At the age of seventy, Phani, herself the victim of outmoded customs, has succeeded in challenging them.

Phaniyamma is a film that deals with female individuality in a male-dominated world circumscribed by immutable laws, conventions and traditions. What Prema Karanth, the director of the film, has sought to do is to call attention to the terrible plight of women in tradition-bound societies and for the need of will power, self-confidence and strength of character to overcome it. Phani, herself a symbol of submission to tradition, becomes a symbol of change as the story unfolds, and the issue of female individuality and identity is at the heart of this film.

Rao Saheb

The second film is Vijaya Mehta's *Rao Saheb* (Barrister, 1986). Mehta has a close relationship with the theatre where she distinguished herself both as a director and an actress. Her first film *Smriti Chitre* won the National Award for the best Marathi-language film of 1983. *Rao Saheb* is her second film. It explores the dualisms of tradition and modernity, inherited custom and social reform as they impinge on the lives of women. Set in the early twentieth century at a time of confrontation between Westernisation and traditional Indian culture, it explores Brahmin orthodoxy, widow remarriage and social reform – all topics that generated much discussion and debate in the 1920s. The film tells the story of a twenty-year old municipal clerk, Bhaurao and his fifteen-year old bride, Radhika. They live in a small outbuilding at the back of a mansion, which has fallen into disrepair. The mansion is owned by Rao Saheb and inhabited by three people who lead strangely isolated lives: Rao Saheb, an English-educated barrister who lives amidst an artificially created Victorian ambience, his brother, Nana Saheb, who is suffering from some mental disorder and has withdrawn into himself and Mawasi, Rao Saheb's aunt who was widowed at the age of ten and leads the austere life of a widow required by custom.

A certain gloominess, both physical and emotional, pervades the mansion and the arrival of the vivacious Radhika infuses new vitality. Mawsi takes a liking to Radhika. Radhika is fascinated by Rao Saheb and his charmingly foreign ways. It is evident that Rao Saheb is nervous and indecisive, caught as he is between two cultures. Meanwhile, Radhika gives birth to a son. Everyone in the household is overjoyed about the arrival of the baby, except the mentally deranged Nana Saheb. One night, in a heavy downpour, he leaves the house to be lost for ever. Bhaurao goes in search of him, but fails to locate him, catches pneumonia and dies soon afterwards.

Tatya, Bhaurao's father, who is given to heavy drinking, blames Rao Saheb for the death of his son and is emphatic that Radhika's hair be shaved off, as prescribed by custom. Rao Saheb, who is constantly harping on the theme of social reform, tries to dissuade Tatya, but he fails. As fate would have it, Tatya drowns in a well. At Rao Saheb's request, Radhika starts to grow her hair and wear bangles, forsakes the austere life of widowhood, and begins to educate herself. The mutual emotional attachment between Rao Saheb and Radhika seems to deepen. Mawsi tells Rao Saheb that he should marry Radhika and he accedes in principle, but cannot bring himself to act. A woman film director has here sought to capture the problems and privations of women from a feminist perspective. *Rao Saheb*, like *Phaniyamma*, touches on the themes of modernity, social change, women's identity, and the power of patriarchy.

36 Chowringhee Lane

The third film is Aparna Sen's *36 Chowringhee Lane* (1981). Aparna Sen has been associated with cinema from very early in life, first gaining critical recognition as an actress in Satyajit Ray's films, and then as a filmmaker in her own right. *36 Chowringhee Lane* is her first film and it deals with the loneliness and disappointments of an Anglo-Indian school teacher. Anglo-Indians led a precarious existence: they adopted British ways of life, wore western clothes, ate Western food, and took Christian names, but they were not considered fully British by the Indians or the British nor fully accepted by either.

One such Anglo-Indian teacher, Violet Stoneham, is the subject of *36 Chowringhee Lane* She is an ageing school teacher, trying to teach Shakespeare to an unappreciative group of girls in Calcutta. She lives on her own in a dark and dingy apartment with a cat for company. Her friends and relatives have all left India for good and all she has are memories. The only person close to her still in India is her brother Eddie who, senile and mentally deranged, is in a home for the aged.

Returning home from church on Christmas day, Violet Stoneham chances to meet Nandita, a former student. Samaresh, Nandita's boyfriend, is with her, and Violet invites them both for coffee. They accept the invitation with some reluctance because the prospect of spending some time with an old woman teacher reminiscing about her past does not particularly appeal to them. However, they quickly realise the possibilities inherent in the situation: they can use Violet's house as a place to meet in privacy rather than using taxi cabs. Samaresh persuades Violet to allow him to use her apartment while she is at school, so that he can write the novel he has long been planning to write in an atmosphere of peace and quiet.

For a while, this arrangement works well for everyone concerned. Samaresh and Nandita are able to spend time together while Violet is in school; and she in turn can return from work to an apartment full of joy and life. A warm and intimate relationship seems to develop between them. Nandita and Samaresh accompany her on walks and bring her dinner from restaurants; she plays old records for their entertainment. Violet's life is again filled with delight, and she even forgets to pay her weekly visit to her brother.

Meanwhile, the atmosphere in school is beginning to turn sour for Violet. A new head of the English department is appointed, a young Indian teacher with the right professional qualifications, but very little experience. Violet is ordered to confine her teaching to English grammar and not teach literature. As her brother becomes more feeble, he grows more irritable. However, Violet is able to face these disappointments and frustrations with equanimity because her intimate relationship with the young Indian couple gives her a much-needed sense of security and human worth. However, that too proves illusory. One day she returns to her apartment unexpectedly and finds out for what purpose the young couple has been using her apartment. Events take a turn for the worse: Eddie dies, and her last link with the Anglo-Indian world is severed. Samaresh lands a job and marries Nandita. As a wedding gift, Nandita's parents give them a fully furnished apartment. Now they have no more use of Violet's apartment. Meeting friends, attending parties and receptions, they very quickly forget Violet.

Violet finds it increasingly difficult to accept the situation. Her misery grows. She pays a visit to the young couple and expresses her hope that their relationship, which means so much to her, will once again flourish. It's Christmas once again; Violet invites Nandita and Samaresh for tea, but they decline, saying that they had made other plans and will be out of town. Violet is greatly disappointed and the film ends with Violet in total and unbearable isolation. The final image of her is on a dark and wet night, all by herself, reciting her favourite Shakespearean lines to a desolate street. Director Aparna Sen has poignantly captured the loneliness of a middle-aged woman, and she does so from within the consciousness of the lonely woman.

Parama

Aparna Sen's *Parama* (1985) also explores female identity in the context of the Indian family and the plight of women as subjects in a culture that tends to marginalise and imprison them. In *Parama*, Sen examines how the identity of women can be rearticulated in terms of the historical experience of gender. The film centres on the life of Parama as she approaches middle age; she married early and lives a sheltered life in a traditional upper-class family. She has absorbed the ethos of orthodox upper-class family living and fastidiously performs the duties expected of her as wife, mother, aunt and sister-in-law. It appears that she has managed totally to submerge her true self in the various roles assigned to her.

A family festival takes place at which Parama plays a crucial role: she is entrusted with overseeing all the details. At this festival, Parama meets the nephew of a friend of her husband's, called Rahul, who earns his living abroad as a photographer. He is visiting India and his passion for recording traditional ceremonies brings him to Parama's house for the festival. Rahul is attracted by Parama although he is much younger than she. As a friend, Rahul would customarily address her as aunt but, instead, he calls her by her first name. Parama finds this somewhat unsettling. Rahul brings to a family gathering the photographs he took at the festival, and Parama is embarrassed to find that she is at the centre of many of them. Her embarrassment grows when her nephew calls to inform her that Rahul wishes to take more photographs of her. At first Parama refuses, but later she agrees when her mother-in-law and the rest of the family convince her that it would be impolite to ignore such a request.

Rahul arrives one morning as Parama is attending to her daily household chores and photographs her. Extremely self-conscious and somewhat troubled by all this, she is relieved when Rahul leaves, saying that he has taken enough photographs. However, Rahul comes back again and asks her to introduce him to the old city. Parama's husband, Bhaskar, is away on business and so, with her mother-in-law's permission, she agrees to accompany him. Parama experiences a new sense of freedom – she finds Rahul's company invigorating. Gradually, she finds herself being emotionally drawn toward Rahul.

In accordance with family custom, Parama has always dutifully played the assigned roles of wife, mother, and daughter-in-law. Now she begins to realise that she is a woman of flesh and blood. Her married life with Bhaskar has settled into a predictable and routine round of events; she takes care of his needs, looks after their children, and maintains a comfortable home. But now she feels desire for Rahul stirring within her; his understanding of her and his pleasant ways appeal to her. Fear overtakes Parama, and she calls up her husband, who is away on business, and asks him to come back immediately. This is not the first time he has been away from home, and as everything seems to be normal, he is surprised by her request. Meanwhile, Parama resolves to be mentally strong and not see Rahul again.

But it happens that Parama meets Rahul by chance in the house of one of her friends. There she yields to her desires and delights in this new relationship; under various subterfuges she gets away from home and spends time with Rahul, A new excitement has entered her life. When Rahul leaves India again, Parama returns to her customary way of life. However, things have changed irretrievably, and neither her husband nor her household seems to have any attraction for her. Rahul writes from abroad, and Parama replies. He specifies a date for his return to India and he sends Parama a magazine featuring some of his photographs of her. On one of the photographs he has penned a message of love. Bhaskar, seeing the magazine, unsuspectingly opens it, and a storm breaks out. Parama's mother disappears to her bedroom and refuses to see her; her husband moves to another room; the children are unwillingly kept away from her; she is no longer allowed to play her earlier important role in the household. She is overcome by unbearable pain. Rahul is presumed lost or stranded in some distant country. Lacking support, Parama decides to take her life.

Parama's family finds her lying bleeding in a bath and rushes her to a nursing home. Her family, somewhat guiltily, gathers around her. She learns that Rahul has been located and is in good health. None of this seems to move Parama. The compassionate family doctor admonishes her that she should seek psychiatric counselling to recover from her trauma and erase her feelings of guilt. Parama's daughter, who had initially condemned her behaviour, now comes and sits by her.

If feminism concerns the recognition of women's predicament of oppression and marginalization because of gender, *Parama* can be described as a film with feminist vision. *Parama* in many ways departs from the standard norms of behaviour and rules of conduct advocated by most Indian films. It is hardly surprising that it generated huge controversy over matters of morality, family life and the changing mores of society.

This consideration of the works of some women filmmakers in India pro-vides some idea of the themes and issues that they deal with. It also dispels the notion that Indian films are monolithically male-centred although the vast majority of popular films made in India do still examine the lives of women from a traditional and male viewpoint, and do portray women as objects of male desire. However, more films are being made which seek to articulate a woman's viewpoint, particularly in the New Indian Cinema.

Feminism and the New Indian Cinema

A fascinating study of the intersection of traditional Indian customs, class and caste structures with feminist issues is Kalpana Lajmi's *Rudaali* (Professional Mourner, 1992). Dimple Kapadia, a glamorous film star, plays the central role of Sanichari the bitter, lonely and hardened woman. She is a bonded labourer to the village landlord who, on his deathbed, summons a professional mourner Bhikni (Raakhee). 'The two women form a bond and Sanichari relates her story (told in flashback) of exploitation and deceit, relieved by moments of joy over her son, who has since abandoned her' (Garga, 1996). Bhikni dies suddenly of cholera but her dying message for Sanichari is that she was the mother who had abandoned her at birth. Sanichari, who has never shed a tear, cries for the first time in her life and becomes a *Rudaali,* one who cries for her living. Combining the social con-cerns of the 'art' cinema with elements of the mass appeal of Bombay films, *Rudaali* contains intriguing elements. For example, Sanichari is highly vul-nerable to all sorts of oppressions. She resists many of them, but succumbs to the dominant discourses. Adapting Marx, one could say that as a woman she makes her own history, but not under conditions of her own choosing. There are a number of instances in the film where the essentialised notions of what it means to be a woman are invoked. When you are watching the film, what do you think of the male protagonists? How does Lajmi, the woman director, portray these?

So far we have made the contrast between popular cinema and art cinema as transparent as possible. We have seen how Indian popular films are made to a formula: concern for the family, reverence for mythological gods and goddesses and the defeat of the criminal as a result of poetic justice. Raina (1986) has drawn attention to how this formulaic narrative, supported by dreamlike visuals and interspersed with music, song and dance, projects our 'deep seated but suppressed fantasies'. The Bombay film, it is alleged, is the opium of the Indian masses. The artistic cinema, however, is to a large extent free from the excesses and the clichés of popular cinema and it 'calls into question some of our psychological and moral values and raises our consciousness about the issues it treats' (Raina 1986: 132) But the art cinema in India remains a minority art and the popular cinema can be read as some of the younger film critics have demonstrated in interesting and novel ways to yield new significances of meaning.

According to Raina (1986), there is a Middle Cinema, one that literally stands between the popular cinema and the élite art cinema. It is aimed at that section of the middle class audience 'who are satisfied with their petty-bourgeois life style and like the comforts of moderately high prosperity...' They are the products of the urban boom, they personalise politics and vote for the Congress Party out of a genuine admiration for the 'dignity and poise' of its leader' (Raina, 1986: 134). Although the Middle cinema tackles important issues, it is their treatment that differentiates this genre from both popular cinema and art cinema. Let us look at some examples.

Sai Paranjpye is a woman director who felt that the distinctions between the two types of cinema were no longer valid. Coming from a theatre and television background, her *Sparsh* (The Touch, 1979) is about Anirudth, the Principal of a school for blind children (played by Naseeruddin Shah) who is himself blind, and his clash with Kavita, (played by Shabana Azmi), a widowed teacher who works in the school. He believes that Kavita is in love with him on account of his blindness. The film is a love story and displays all the clichés of love stories in the popular cinema – 'the opening and closing songs, the stretches of visuals in which the lovers are shown in idyllic surroundings ...' The film won three National Awards and although it treats the issue of blindness without sentimentality, it does not delve deeply enough into the position of the blind (disabled) in a country like India.

Mahesh Bhatt's *Arth* (The Meaning, 1983) is about a middle class urban marriage on the verge of collapse. The husband leaves his wife to live with an artist but returns to his wife, who rejects him. This act of defiance appeals to middle class educated women who saw in the film glimmerings of protest 'against a duplicitous sexual code which condemns a woman for infractions of the marriage covenant, but condones similar lapses by men' (Raina, 1986:137). However, the 'injured' wife sets up house with her maid servant's daughter, whose mother too is maltreated by her drunken husband. The fact that the wife does not seek sexual fulfilment through another lover ensures the status quo and there is no exploration of the social and psychological factors that make for marital discord.

In *Masoom* (The Innocent, 1983), the peaceful life of a couple is 'shattered by the arrival of a small boy, the illegitimate son of the husband'. This film is a recycled version of Kramer Vs Kramer and Shekhar Kapur's (the director) handling of the theme is considered to be gentle and deft. Similar to the situation in popular films, the affair between the husband and the boy's mother is shown in flashbacks with the usual floral surroundings. However, the film side-steps the thorny issue of the status of the unwed mother in middle class society. Furthermore, as Rajadhyaksha and Willemen (1994:423) observe, the film also side-steps 'the knottier aspects of the problem by making the illegitimate child a boy and by requiring the wife to accept the fruit of her husband's infidelity rather that the other way around'.

Finally, in this Middle cinema genre, we can look at *Chakra* (The Wheel, 1980). Directed by Rabindra Dharmaraj (who died at the age of 33), it depicts life among Bombay's slumdwellers and predates Nair's *Salaam Bombay* (1988) by a few years. Amma (Smita Patil) and her son Benwa (Ranjit Choudhury) move into the squalor of a tenement in Bombay after her husband killed a money lender who tried to rape her. The husband was then shot for trying to steal some tin to build a hut. As Raina (1986:135) perceptively commented: 'the wheel of this woman's fate keeps revolving, is never steady and uproots her from not only her habitat but also her dreams'. Elements of popular cinema are again present – for example, the 'heroine's sexuality is made an object for the leering camera-eye, as in the bathing-scene'. But with such predictable cinematic strategies, this film also fails to address properly the problem of the underclass.

Women Filmmakers in Mumbai in the New Millennium
A path has been hewn by women directors and others are moving along it. In mid 2003, scriptwriter Honey Irani made her debut as a director with *Armaan* (Desire), starring Amitabh Bachchan, Anil Kapoor, Preity Zinta and Gracy Singh. No woman working in Bollywood had ever had the luxury of directing such a star cast as this. Later that year women directors in Mumbai gained further recognition. Of the six Bollywood films released over two weeks in September, 2003, three were directed by women.

Parvati Balagopalan's directorial debut, *Rules: Pyaar Ka Superhit Formula* made quite an impact with its story of a young girl smitten by a top male model. Shona Urvashi tried her luck with the romantic comedy *Chupke Se...* (Furtively), which revolved around the ecstasies and heartbreaks of a middle class girl with stars in her eyes.

Also in 2003, Kalpana Lajmi (see pages 83 and 90) produced *Kyon* (Why?). This looked at the dangers inherent in the permissiveness and consumerist frenzy that 'Generation X youngsters' indulge in in metropolitan India but it was shoddily mounted and did poorly at the box office. In 2000, Lajmi directed *Daman* (Repression), about a bruised and battered woman in a feudal Assamese household who avenges the indignities heaped on her by assuming the *avatar* of the Mother Goddess Durga and impaling her husband on a trident. This too failed at the box office.

In 2002, Revathi, the star of a string of Tamil and Telugu hits, made waves with her first film as director. *Mitr My Friend* had an all-woman technical crew, including the cinematographer Fowzia and editor Bina Venugopal. It was about a non-resident Indian (NRI – 'A non-resident Indian is a person of Indian origin recognised by the Indian state... as residing outside India, and on whom it bestows special financial privileges with expectation of foreign exchange investments in India...' Virdi, 2003: 241) who bonds with a man – the *Friend* of the title – whom she befriends in an Internet chat room. Revathi plans a more ambitious project still, in which Abhishek Bachchan is tipped to play the male lead.

At the time of writing, other women are making their directorial debuts. Choreographer Farah Khan managed to assemble an enviable star cast – Shahrukh Khan, Sushmita Sen, Zayed Khan, Amrita Rao and Sunil Shetty – for her first film *Main Hoon Na* (Bank on Me), while actress and producer Pooja Bhatt had John Abraham and Udita Goswani in the lead roles for her film *Paap* (Sin).

Is the Bollywood film industry's attitude towards women directors really changing? It is clear that women directors who have carved a niche for themselves over the years have built their careers almost entirely on funding from the West or have worked in regional cinemas.

Successes achieved by women filmmakers in Mumbai have been sporadic at best. Sai Paranjpye (see page 91) and Vijaya Metha (see pages 69 and 85) have not lived up to the expectations raised by their earlier films. The exception here is Aparna Sen, who followed her well-crafted *36 Chowringhee Lane* and *Parama* (see pages 86-88) with *Mr and Mrs Iyer* in 2002. Aparna Sen's daughter, Konkona won the National Award for Best Actress for *Mr and Mrs Iye,* and the film has won accolades at major film festivals. Aparna Sen is currently working on a Hindi film *Gulel,* starring Ajay Devgan, Saif Ali Khan, Kareena Kapoor and Bipasha Basu.

Interestingly, few of the women directors making films in Hindi specifically address gender issues. Many would appear to resist the feminist label, probably feeling that this would limit the scope of their work. One exception is *Filhaal* (For the Moment). Meghna Gulzar's directorial debut looks like a designer film – diligently created backdrops, classy colour schemes, elegantly attired actors and a slick narrative methodology which has a pleasantly relaxed air – and it hinges on real emotions. *Filhaal* is about life – about four lives, in fact. Two city girls, Rewa (Tabu) and Sia (Sushmita Sen), who are poles apart temperamentally, have grown up together. Rewa is obsessed with marriage and motherhood, while Sia, a fashion photographer, is committed to her professional career. A fencing accident renders Rewa incapable of sustaining a pregnancy beyond a few months, so when she has a miscarriage a year after marrying garment trader Dhruv (Sanjay Suri), her world crumbles. Sia, who has steadfastly thwarted persistent marriage proposals from her boyfriend Saahil (Palash Sen), offers to nurture the next baby Rewa conceives in her own womb. The concept of female bonding reaches a level no Hindi film has attained before, as the two women defy the misgivings of their families to give the bold experiment a shot. But, as they discover, it's not all plain sailing – a streak of insecurity grips Rewa and this engenders such jealousy and possessiveness that it threatens to tear the two friends apart...

Sadly, *Filhaal* did not succeed commercially. Not only did this slow Meghna Gulzar down – she is now reported to be scripting a new film to be set on the Indo-Pakistan border – but it also discouraged women filmmakers even more about mining explicit feminist themes for their films.

CHAPTER 6

Styles and Techniques

At one level, cinema is a universal art form, transcending its locality. At another level, it depends for its success on being grounded in a specific culture and drawing on its resources. Hollywood Westerns, samurai films of Japan, martial arts films of Hong Kong and the romantic musicals of India all illustrate this. This chapter focuses on the distinctiveness of Indian popular cinema.

In terms of style and techniques of presentation, Indian popular cinema is in sharp contrast to artistic films, which are generally realistic and follow the neo-realistic tradition, exploring social problems and inequities. According to Rinki Roy Bhattacharya (in personal communication), the polarisation between commercial and artistic cinema occurred in the 1960s when renowned directors such as Guru Dutt (1965), Mehboob Khan (1965) and Bimal Roy (1966) were replaced by a new breed of directors, mainly graduates of the Pune Film Institute or film society members. Notable in this emerging group (some already discussed here) and claiming parallel status were Basu Chatterjee (cartoonist in the tabloid *Blitz*), Basu Bhattacharya (assistant briefly to Bimal Roy), Mani Kaul, Kumar Sahani (graduates of Pune Institute), Shyam Benegal (from the advertisement media), Ritwik Ghatak (who scripted Bimal Roy's *Madhumati* and was a Professor of Film Direction), Adoor Gopalakrishnan (from Kerala) and Mrinal Sen (who worked as an apprentice in sound recording studio). Bhattacharya's debut film, *Teesri Kasam* (The Third Vow, 1965) was a breath of fresh air in the void left by the previous directors. A delicate love story, it won the award for best Hindi film of 1965. However, according to Rinki Roy Bhattacharya, none of his works was considered 'new wave' except *Uski Kahani* (His/Her Story, 1966). To qualify for the new wave genre ('a label thrust upon this group, indicating the European nouvelle vogue') it was obligatory for the film to be low budget, songless and starless. These were the identification marks, at least in the formative stage. However, Ritwik Ghatak and Mrinal Sen, whose contributions we discuss below, are firmly located within the new wave cinema.

No better contrast between the commercial success of Indian popular cinema and the box-office failures of some of the artistic films could be found than Ritwik Ghatak's films. His films were not 'hits' and his genius has only quite recently been acknowledged. As one commentator (Levich, 1997:30-32) says:

> Each work is a work of genuine distinction, marked by formal daring, intellectual vigor, and powerful persuasion. At least two of them – The Cloud-Capped Star (*Meghe Dhaka Tara*, 1960) and *Subarnarekha* (1965) are acknowledged masterpieces whose stature has only increased with time.

Ghatak used melodrama in the service of high art; he made his sound tracks 'thick'; anti-naturalistic sound and eccentric focal techniques combined with his Marxist politics. But in his use of melodrama, he harked back to the Indian theatre traditions and mythical archetypes. These enabled him to satisfy his longing for his roots so as to cope with seeing his homeland, Bengal, become part of Pakistan in 1947. Hence his preoccupation with Partition and its terrible aftermath.

Mrinal Sen's influence is of a different order. His *Bhuvan Shome* (1969) –considered to be the origin of the New Indian cinema – has influenced a whole generation of filmmakers. Made on a tiny budget, *Bhuvan Shome* won the award of Best Film, Best Director and Utpal Dutt for Best Actor. Sen is generally 'regarded as the leading proponent of political cinema in India' (Vasudev, 1995:75). He is a craftsman and his experimenting with cinematic expression has earned acclaim, but time has also worked in his favour. *Bhuvan Shome* was released in 1969 when the Indian cinema was poised for change – the old order of Mehboob Khan, Bimal Roy, Guru Dutt and even Raj Kapoor was being replaced and there was a cast of almost entirely new faces – Utpal Dutt, Sushasini Mulay, Shekhar Chatterjee, Sadhu Meher and even Amitabh Bachchan to help with narration (see Mukhopadhyay 1995 chapter 4, for a comprehensive account of the film's ground-breaking nature).

Most were shot not in studios but in real locations. *Bhuvan Shome* was financed by a government agency, the FFC (Film Finance Corporation). According to Rinki Roy Bhattacharya, however, the FFC did not provide distribution for the new wave films and they were seldom granted the normal schedule of three shows per day. So even with funding, there was no distribution back-up to market the films. Sen's films, like Ghatak's, were not commercial successes. According to Mukhopadhyay (1995), Goswamy, who backed Sen's *Mahaprithivi* (Great World, 1991) later remarked: 'I would never approach an art film-walla anymore. If I make a film, I shall be out-and-out commercial'. What, then, makes Indian popular films commercially successful?

Stylisation and Popular Cinema

The popular films are mostly romantic musicals that offer escapism and fantasy worlds to the movie goers. Entertainment is their watchword. Although it is unwise to lump all popular films into a single category or to ignore their historical evolution, one can fairly identify certain characteristics in them.

In Chapter One we identified six major influences that shaped Indian popular cinema. All relate not only to content but also to the characteristic style and techniques of presentation. The first was the epics the *Ramayana* and the *Mahabharata* and their profound influence on the thought and imagination of the peoples of India and on its cinema. The art of narrative clearly owes much to the epics and particularly, to their structure. There is a circular pattern in which narratives are embedded in other narratives. Indian popular films reflect this since their narrative is rarely linear – plots branch off into sub-plots. Good examples of these narrative dispersals can be found in *Khalnayak* (1993) and *Gardish* (1993) and these two films also illustrate the changing narrative strategies of the nineties, on which we elaborate in the next chapter.

Second is the impact of classical Sanskrit theatre in Indian popular films. We have already drawn attention to its highly stylised nature and its emphasis on spectacle. In classical theatre, music, dance and gesture combine magnificently to create a vibrant artistic unit with dance and mime being central to the dramatic experience. The Sanskrit word *natya* meaning drama is derived from the root *nrit*, to dance. One can characterise Sanskrit dramas as spectacular dance-dramas and this has carried over into Indian popular films.

The influence of Sanskrit theatre was not conveyed to the cinema directly but was channelled through the regional folk-theatres of India. After the tenth century, Sanskrit theatre declined and the regional folk theatres that sprang up retained many of its stylistic elements. Through folk dramas like Yatra of Bengal, Ram Lila of Uttar Pradesh, Terukkuttu of Tamilnadu classical theatre affected popular films – the third formative influence.

The fourth was the Parsi theatre. The plays blended realism and fantasy, music and dance, narrative and spectacle, earthy dialogue and ingenuity of stage presentation, integrating them within a dramatic discourse of melodrama. The Parsi plays contained crude humour, melodious songs and music, sensationalism and dazzling stagecraft. All these elements fascinated theatre-goers who saw drama as a form of undemanding entertainment. The Parsi plays powerfully influenced Indian popular films. The styles and techniques that we associate with the popular cinema can be traced in large measure to them.

Fifthly, the impact of Hollywood is clearly discernible in Indian popular films. Its technical ingenuity appealed to Indian filmmakers, and Hollywood musicals stirred their imaginations. Hollywood musicals achieved their high point in the 1920s to the 1950s and Indian film directors were quick to draw on them for their own musicals, but with some differences in approach already discussed. For example, the Hollywood musicals had as their plot the world of entertainment itself. Indian filmmakers, while enhancing the elements of fantasy so pervasive in Indian popular films, used song and music as a natural mode of articulation in a given situation in their films. There is a strong Indian tradition of narrating mythology, history, fairy stories and so on through song and dance.

The Indian filmmakers departed from their Hollywood counterparts in another way: whereas Hollywood filmmakers strove to conceal the constructed nature of their work so that the realistic narrative was wholly dominant, Indian filmmakers made no attempt to conceal the fact that what was shown on the screen was a creation, an illusion, a fiction. However, they demonstrated how this creation intersected with people's day to day lives in complex and interesting ways.

Finally, the impact of Western musical television (MTV) is being increasingly felt in Indian films: their pace, the camera angles, the music, the dance sequences. One has only to see Mani Rathnam's *Bombay*, a popular and controversial film to realise this. These six cultural forces have shaped the style and techniques of Indian popular cinema.

A number of elements invest Indian popular cinema with a clear identity. Among these are the following:

* Indian popular films are not realistic in the strictest sense

* They seek to create a world of fantasy

* Acting is exaggerated

* All aspects of the filmic experience are melodramatic

* The use of the camera is often flashy, drawing attention to itself

* Editing is very obtrusive

* Stereotypes related to character and situation are common

* Music is central

* Songs, very often sung by well-known playback signers, are crucial in unfolding the narrative

* Dance sequences are often used to intensify the intended emotions and the spectacle

Indian popular films never pretend to be wholly realistic. The stories may be filmed in a realistic setting, but the styles of presentation are products of cultural stylisation – for instance, the way music, song and dance are deployed. Audiences are perfectly willing to accept that the hero or heroine when anxious could break into song or that they dance gaily when happy. Audiences perceive no disjuncture between the story with its realistic, everyday setting and the song and dance sequences. This is primarily because they have come to accept that films are governed by conventions commonly shared between them and the filmmakers and audiences. These conventions have evolved over time and have reached a measure of stability. Indian popular films cannot be judged by the realistic yardsticks applied to Western films. Each needs to be understood and evaluated in terms of their conventions. The style and techniques of Indian popular cinema are highly stylised.

Glamour and Overstatement
To create a world of fantasy, sets are elaborate and glittering, whether the films be religious or contemporary social dramas. The elaborate sets of the religious and mythological films are associated with royal courts or heavenly abodes. Social dramas could be set in glamorous nightclubs or upper-class mansions. One of the goals of these popular films is to provide viewers with easy routes to worlds of fantasy. The exaggeration and flashiness provide temporary satisfaction in these fantasy worlds and brief escape from the miseries and privations of daily life.

Many Indian popular films are both romantic musicals and melodramas. The fundamental trait of the melodramas is excess – the emotion is always in excess of what the situation demands and this is reinforced by both the acting style and the modes of presentation. Melodrama tends to simplify the world and present everything in stark contrasts. And this is what Indian popular cinema does.

Flashiness and exuberance characterise Indian popular cinema. Camera angles and the use of close-ups serve to call attention to the ingenuity of cameramen, quite apart from their function in advancing the story. Similarly, the editing, unlike in Hollywood films, is intentionally obtrusive although this is not to say that editors do not display any imagination or ingenuity.

Stereotypical Characterisation
Also distinctive is the representation of stereotyped characters. The heroes, heroines, villains and comedians are readily identifiable. Their demeanour, dress and gestures are highly conventionalised and immediately convey the nature of the character. It is useful to note how two comedians see their styles

and techniques. Comedian Jagdeep is well-known for his role as the pick-pocket shoe-shine man in Bimal Roy's *Do Bigha Zamin* (Two Acres of Land, 1953). His style and technique, according to Rinki Roy Bhattacharya (daughter of Bimal Roy), defies fixed labels. Unlike Johnny Walker, Jagdeep's face is 'serious' and he uses every trick in the trade – facial contortions, loud guffaws, bursting into song or into tears, body language – to convey his art. Comparing the situation with what he did in the fifties, Jagdeep complains that many directors now go for cheap jokes and, worst of all, lines already written are changed overnight at the whims of a star or director.

Johnny Walker has acted in more than 300 films in a long and successful career which includes *Pyaasa* (1957), *CID* (1956), *Sahib Bibi Aur Ghulam* (Master, Mistress, Slave, 1962), *Madhumati* (1958), *Chaudhvin Ka Chand* (Full Moon, 1960), *Taxi Driver* (1954) and *Anand* (1970). His mannerisms and his comic drunken sequences are legendary, and his biggest asset is his face. He says that when people look at him, they begin laughing. In many of his films he made last-minute changes in order to maximise the humour. And he is also remembered for fronting certain memorable songs (sung by playback singer Mohammed Rafi): *Tel Maalish (Pyaasa), Ye hai bambai meri jaan (CID)* and *Jaane Kahan Mera jigar gaya ji (Mr and Mrs 55)*. Like some of the music directors, he opted out of the 1970s and early 1980s film scene because he felt that comedy had lost its charm. But he is making a come-back in the film *Sree 420* in the role of a make-up man (see *Sunday Mid-day* part 2, June 29, 1997 for a longer discussion of the return of Johnny Walker).

Music, Song and Dance Sequences
Barnouw and Krishnaswamy (1963) suggest why music and song are so popular in Indian cinema :

a) they are linked to the regional theatre of the nineteenth century, which made great use of song

b) music provides the catalyst in a country with huge linguistic diversity. Whereas regional theatres were language-based, films tended to be culture-based. Music and mythology provided common cultural bonds between the North and the South of India.

Music, song and dance have traditionally played an integral role in the daily life of Indian peoples, whether for religious and devotional purposes or for celebrations such as birthdays and weddings. So the music, song and dance sequences in the first Indian sound films were seen as natural by Indian audiences. Furthermore, since many early Hindi films were filmed staged plays, 'film music directors transplanted music and dance from the theatre to the screen.' (Arnold, 1991).

The popularity of many films depends largely on how much its music appeals to movie-goers. In the first Hindi films, as Arnold (1991) has observed, songs were used to enhance the drama rather than develop story lines. Later on, some film and music directors such as Raj Kapoor and Naushad in the 1950s, 'used film songs as an extension of the dialogue to convey story and dramatic action' (Arnold, 1991).

Music, then, fulfils a number of functions in Indian cinema. Firstly, it is a vital element of the film experience. A film is unlikely to attain mass popularity if it has no songs; indeed, long after the story of the film has been forgotten, its songs live on in the imagination of people. Secondly, songs are used for specific purposes. They help to intensify the emotions associated with a given situation; they serve to underline moral sentiments and they play an important role in generating eroticism where sexual explicitness is forbidden on screen. Indeed, it is difficult to say whether successful films owe their success to their songs or vice versa. One reason why few artistic films enjoy commercial success is because there are no songs – without them the 'average' Indian movie-goer finds films boring.

Music and songs are used as tools of narration, and there are songs for every mood and emotion – romantic, sad, devotional, patriotic, cabaret, comical or simply lullabies. But there is no compartmentalisation here – there is much crossover. Whether it be Dev Anand singing in *Guide* (1965) or *Kala Bazar* (Black Market, 1960) or Raj Kapoor in *Barsaat* (Rain 1949), devotional or sad songs are used for the romantic situations.

However, in the words of Kabir and Snell (1994:219): 'the popular music of India comes from the cinema screen, out of the mouths of the actors and actresses whose singing voices belong to invisible performers – the 'playback singers' or dubbing artists...' Playback singing dates back to the 1930s when technological developments allowed sound and picture to be recorded independently, enabling the separation of the performer on the visual film track from the singer on the sound track. Playback singing led to changes in singing styles. Singers such as K.L.Saigal, Surendra, Pahari Sanyal, Nurjehan and Suraiya were also actors and actresses; Saigal, for example, was 'untrained in classical music, yet his style of singing was in the classical mode' (Kabir, 1991).

A new style emerged when playback singers had to adapt their voices to suit the different screen characters for whom they sang. As Arnold (1991) put it:

this technique involved not only changing vocal styles, musical styles, and pronunciation of the lyrics to match Hindu and Muslim, North Indian, South Indian, upper class and lower class screen characters, but also varying vocal range to suit old and young characters.

Some playback singers have, however, become associated not only with certain musical styles but also with specific actors/actresses. Although Lata Mangeskhar (who appears in the Guinness Book of Records as the world's most recorded artist) is extremely versatile and has sung for a variety of actresses, Mukesh's voice seems for audiences to be the voice of actor/director Raj Kapoor, who once said that 'Mukesh's voice is the voice of my soul' (Kabir and Snell, 1994:220).

Saigal's influence on singers was significant and so was the ghazal form in which he sang. The *ghazal* is a light classical Indian song form originating in Persia (Iran). The Persian *ghazal* gradually gave way to the Urdu *ghazal*, which enjoys prodigious popularity in North India and Pakistan. As Manuel (1993:90) observes: 'Although Urdu is, on the whole, a product of Indo-Muslim culture, the *ghazal* has traditionally been enjoyed and cultivated by Hindus as well.' Herein lies one of the significant contributions of Indian popular cinema to Indian society. Since linguistic diversity has been the most formidable barrier to the development of a subcontinental pop music, Indian film songs have synthesised a variety of musical elements including bhajans, qawwalis, Latin American and Western ones to create an essentially national Hindi genre. Much of the credit for this must go to talented music composers such as Naushad and S.D. Burman. According to Kabir and Snell (1994:221), in the 1950s established poets such as Shailendra and Kaifi Azmi wrote for the cinema, raising the level of the film song to a form of poetry. This national music, particularly as reflected in the 1940s, 1950s, and 1960s 'succeeded in uniting India's people where politics, economics, social class and religion have all failed' (Arnold, 1988). We pick up this success story of music in Chapter Seven.

Diasporic influences on music in Indian films
Indian popular cinema is drawing on the influence of diaspora and particularly its music and reflecting their cultural developments back to them.

The involvement of the Muslim communities in Britain in Indian popular cinema is increasingly evident but Pakistan is producing more films and their international stars now feature on Zee TV in Britain. The role of music in the

Muslim communities in Britain is particularly intriguing, as Baily's (1995) research on the role of music in certain British Muslim communities reveals. Although the majority of British Muslims come from South Asia, there are considerable differences among them. Baily (1995:77) identifies three main groups: the Mirpus from Azad Kashmir in Pakistan, Khalifas from Gujarat in India and Afghans chiefly from Kabul.

Only the Mirpus appear to be indifferent to music; although they enjoy it in the Hindi and Urdu movies which, according to Baily (1995), they watch on their home videos or hear on Sunrise Radio. The Khalifas are substantially involved in music, particularly Indian popular music.

> Several of the most prominent Asian professional musicians living in London are Khalifas, often seen as accompanists on BBC Asian music television programmes. Naya Saz, Sargam, Khilona Arts and Diwana Arts are examples of predominantly Khalifa bands in Britain. They play a highly amplified vision of film *git* ... (Baily, 1995:82).

Afghans are also heavily involved in music, the kind that prevails in Indian popular cinema. Kabul's radio and TV station have been destroyed and Afghan musicians in Britain are intent on re-creating their music of some 25 years ago. Baily (1995) reports that the Society of Afghan Residents in the UK has organised concerts of Afghan music with visiting Afghan artists such as woman singer Ustad Mahevash. To some extent Afghan music in Britain seems to have been inspired 'by the popularity of bhangra music among other South Asian communities in Britain' (Baily, 1995).

Bhangra, originally a male form of rural folk music and dance from the North Western state of Punjab, was brought to Britain by Punjabi immigrants in the 1950s and 1960s. It celebrates *baisakhi* (the Punjabi new year) and the bringing in of the harvest.

> In keeping with the character of the people, it is vibrant, rhythmic and joyfully hedonistic and the language in which it is sung has been described as the 'cockney of India' (Banerji, 1988).

Bhangra musicians perform at religious and social functions all over Britain. The first generation of Bhangra musicians probably used the music to develop a sense of Asianness in the midst of the racism they faced. Channi, the lead singer of Alaap, the first group to popularise bhangra in South Asian British communities in the late 1970s, says:

> We noticed that young Punjabis in London knew little about their own culture and language and were immersed in the English disco scene. We

started our bhangra songs to bring them back into their own culture. But for the music to appeal to them, we had to add the western touch with a drum beat and synthesisers. (quoted by Gopinath, 1995:309)

Since the 1980s bhangra music has drawn upon other forms of music such as reggae, house and soul. Two of the best known singers are Apache Indian and Sagoo. Apache Indian uses reggae and Jamaican patois and Sagoo mixes traditional Sufi devotional songs with rap and reggae and both of them have achieved international fame. The issue of fusion and fission is discussed on page 120.

The popularisation of Qawwali, the musical form of the Sufi mystic tradition, is due mainly to Nusrat Fateh Ali Khan, who created a new kind of music by using Western musical instruments and fusing the traditional with the modern. Qawwali is a derivative of the world *qol* – the saying; it is rhythm-oriented and has a distinctive style. What Nusrat did was to increase the tempo and improvise by repeating phrases often in complex rhythmic patterns to produce an ecstatic, trance-like effect. Although he was criticised by fundamentalist critics in Pakistan, he was attracted to the East-West fusion and his voice was used in Gabriel's soundtrack for *The Last Temptation* (1988) and a string of albums for Gabriel's label, including *Shahbaaz* (1991) and *The Last Prophet* (1994). He also composed the score for *Bandit Queen* (1995).

Dance

With regard to dance, the story is rather different. Like music and songs, dance sequences are part of the formula of 'one or two stars, six songs and three dances' in every film – which still persists. But unlike music and songs, dance sequences are not always integrated into the main story.

This is due chiefly to the origins of dance itself. In Phalke's *Raja Harischandra* (1913), all the women's parts were played by men, but ultimately Phalke succeeded in persuading Kamala, a stage actress, to dance in his film *Mohini Bhasmasur* (1913). Ramchandran (1985:253) describes this dance: 'God Vishnu, incarnating as temptress Mohini, lured the demon Bhasmasur to his doom through a seductive dance'. The dancing, choreographed by Phalke himself, originated from sources that included stone carvings of temples, paintings on the walls of Ajanta caves and from Devadasi dances and 'Tamasha' (Western Indian Folk) dancing.

In its long history, dance (together with drama) was once esteemed as a sacred art. Indeed, Shiva is one of the most familiar figures of all Hindu deities as Lord of the Dance and figures of him as a male dancer, with one foot in the air, surrounded by a ring of flame, are sold in tourist shops all over India. The Devadasis – servants of the goddess – performed Bharat Natyam, a southern Indian dance form associated with the temple, while Khatak (storyteller) dance was used with music in the temples of North India as a means of conveying to the people the myths of the gods.

In the eyes of respectable society, the Devadasis were increasingly reduced to *dasis*, mere prostitutes/slaves (see Bharucha 1995 for a comprehensive account). Serious attempts were made, particularly in the 1940s, to present a complete dance film, largely as the result of Uday Sankar's efforts to rehabilitate the classical dance. *Kalpana* (Dream, 1948) crowned his efforts, but the film didn't appeal to the masses and the 'Indian cinema had failed to evolve and develop a dance-cum-musical film as a distinct genre' (Ramachandran, 1985:248).

The 1940s also saw the development of some hybrid forms of dancing which became very popular. *Jhanak Jhanak Payal Baaje* (Jangle, Jangle, Sound the Bells, 1948) had spectacular dance numbers on a variety of ancient themes. Mumtaz Ali composed most of the dances in the Bombay talkies which were singularly successful. His most famous dance spectacles were *Main Dilli Dulham Caje Re*, (*Jhoola*, 1941) *Jawanee Kee Rail Ghadi Jaye* (*Shenaz*, 1947) and *Chana Jor Gharain Babu Main Laya Majedar* (*Bandhan*, 1940). Shashi Deo, an Indian choreographer who lives in London, told us that Mumtaz Ali used simple dance steps

> ...of turning, bending and wide hand and arms gestures for his compositions. Most of this kind of dance was a chase and tease of male and female turn, similar to British music hall acts which were then very popular in British films, with sexual overtones in words and movements

Another form of dancing was popularised by Vyjayanthimala who, in the film *New Delhi* (1956), combined Bharat Nayam dance steps with Khatak dance and Bhangra, a Punjabi folk dance. What became especially popular, however, was cabaret dancing where Western, mainly Anglo-Indian, dancers like Cuckoo and Helen achieved stardom in their own right. Cabaret dancing, however, reminds us of Aruna Vasudev's comment that women are portrayed as either vamps or victims. In Indian cinema this form of dancing exemplifies the objectification of woman: she is a spectacle, par excellence – a body to be looked at, the locus of sensuality, an object of desire.

Another form of dancing is used as part of the courtesan films genre. Chandra (1973) tells us that prostitution was well established and respected in ancient India. Chakravarty (1996:277) uses the terms courtesan and prostitute interchangeably and remarks that 'a complex picture emerges of an institution that was prevalent in all parts of India and toward which moral opprobrium existed side by side with widespread social acceptance'. Nonetheless, the 'courtesan films' have been instrumental in the careers of some famous actresses including Meena Kumari, Vyjayantimala, Sharmila Tagore and Rekha. *Pakeeza* (The Pure One, 1971) and *Umrao Jan* (1981) illustrate some of the significant aspects of the courtesan film. *Pakeeza*, a classic, starred Meena Kumari and was a huge box office hit. As Chakravarty (1996: 291) notes: '*Pakeeza* is poetry and fantasy and nostalgia all orchestrated together on a grand scale'. *Umrao Jan* is rated as the quintessential courtesan film of the Bombay cinema. Starring Rekha, the film 'constructs a visual and musical treat through its social tapestry, lavish sets, personalised star appeal, romantic drama, and pathos' (Chakravarty, 1996:287).

Both *Pakeeza* and *Umrao Jan* draw upon Muslim culture and here again, as in the case of music and songs, the fusion of Muslim and Hindu elements, particularly in terms of the ghazals sung by Asha Bhonsle and the use of Urdu, is an important part of Hindu-Muslim unity, and so of Indian nationhood.

How Films are Made

From an Idea or a Novel to the Screen

Director and screenplay writer together discuss the characterization of the story. Next, they plot the progression: the start, middle and end. It is not necessary to remain faithful to a given novel or original story; director and writer are free to mould a story into a visual form to be translated onto film. The stages indicated overleaf are generally applicable to the Indian context.

Stages by which films in India are made

1 Story selected by the producer or producer/director or even an actor.

2 Screenplay writer and director together translate chosen story into cinematic form.

3 Even before final draft, the dialogue writer enters and works with director, to give it spoken expression. This helps edit out repetitions and continues to make dramatic progression.

4 Budget is discussed with executive producer. Screenplay adjusted if necessary to suit the budget.

5 Main actors and actresses are cast.

6 Financier and distributors come in once cast is known. They hear the story line. In Indian films today, they virtually dictate to the director how many songs and dances there should be in the film.

7 Entire technical unit is contracted, including music director.

8 Dates are booked for the shoot. It may take six months to three and half years to complete, depending on the stars involved and the flow of money.

9 The editor views the rushes as ready, and when it fits with other films simultaneously being edited.

10 Editor makes rough cut of all that is filmed. During gaps in shooting, the director sees rough cut, makes alterations where necessary. Financier and distributors are given screenings before they hand over further money.

11 Once film is shot, edited, viewed, discussed again and again, re-edited to suit all sorts of demands from the stars, financier and distributors, final cut is made. First married print is struck.

12 Film is shown to Board of Film Censors, which often requests changes before issuing certificate. Requisite changes made by editor in conjunction with director.

13 Music composer is shown finished film and composes music for entire film. Background is recorded.

14 Editor fits recorded background music to film, and fits in all sound effects.

15 Film is re-recorded.

16 Release print is struck.

17 Press shows are held. (Pre-release press shows and reviews are extremely important).

18 After a massive publicity campaign, the film is finally released for general release.

Source: Amit Bose (personal communication).

CHAPTER 7

The Changing Scene in Indian Popular Cinema

The introduction to this updated survey of Indian cinema focused on the historical and cultural impact of globalisation on Indian popular cinema, particularly Bollywood. In this chapter we map the contours of contemporary Hindi cinema, which over the past twelve years has been shaped largely by four interrelated developments: economic, social, political and technological.

Economically, India is expected by the year 2020 to be the fourth largest economy in the world in terms of purchasing power parity. The ground for this dramatic U-turn was laid partly by the liberalisation and globalisation policies of the minority Congress government of Narasimha Rao in the early 1990s. With the fall of the Soviet Union, India severed all links with the Soviet industrial model and Soviet patronage and Narasimha Rao's government introduced substantial fiscal, industrial and agricultural policies and achieved significant results. Economic progress has been partly driven by the government's back-to-back five-year plans that began in 1951.

Socially, the opening up of the once protected economy precipitated a surge in consumerist tendencies. The growth in the number of the middle classes in India has been documented (*inter alia* by Dubey, 1992; Varma, 1998; National Council of Applied Economic Research, 1998; Page and Crawley, 2001; Gokulsing, 2004). According to some estimates,

- the Indian middle classes are estimated to number between 100-200 million depending on how they are identified

- the Indian middle classes consist of professionals, salaried employees of state bureaucracies, small-scale entrepreneurs, traders and prosperous farmers, and represented households earning annual incomes of between 400 US dollars and 1867 US dollars (Mankekar, 1999: 75).

Page and Crawley (2001: 111) identify a number of distinct classes by their patterns of consumption rather than their income and this typology categorises nearly half the population of India – about 400 million – as having consumer power (See Dwyer, 2000: Chapter 3 for a useful analysis of the middle classes of Bombay).

Politically, the secular nationalism which prevailed from the Partition to the 1970s has been challenged by a Hindu nationalism expressed in the Bharatiya Janata Party's (BJP) *Hindutva* doctrine – a clear-cut identity based on nationalism and patriotism. The explicit mission of the BJP and its associates is 'to get even with history and to develop a particular notion of Indianness and, more importantly, a particular notion of the Hindu' (Gokulsing, 2004). The agenda has been considerably enhanced by the telecasting of the *Ramayan* and the *Mahabharat* on Doordarshan in the 1980s.

Technologically, the advent of satellite channels in the early 1990s – CNN, ZeeTV, Star, Sony, Sun – has accelerated the pace of globalisation. The new style programmes include popular and influential western-style soap operas on Doordarshan and the satellite channels. The Indian audience is now in a global village, exposed to programmes of the kind viewed in western countries.

The impact of these developments on contemporary Indian cinema can be categorised as follows:

* the partial eclipse of films based on corruption and taking the law into your hands – films that caused the meteoric rise of Amitabh Bachchan in the 1970s and 1980s

* the return of the song and dance formula and family entertainment orientation, with carefully choreographed song and dance extravaganzas, as in

  Hum Aapke Hain Koun!
  Dilwale Dulhania Le Jayenge
  Dil To Pagal Hai (The Heart is a Wild Thing, 1997)
  Kuch Kuch Hota Hai
  Khabi Khushi Kabbie Gham (Joys and Sorrows, 2001)

* an increasing number of films with national and patriotic themes that reflect the rise to political power of the BJP. These include *Roja* (1992); *Sardar* (1993); *Bombay* (1994); *Sarfarosh* (The Rebel, 1999); *Refugee*

(2000); *Mission Kashmir* (2000) and *Gadar – Ek Prem Katha* (Uprising, A Love Story, 2001)

- the new status of the Indian film industry that now has access to banking facilities and insurance cover

- scripts increasingly becoming the basis for a film, in place of the star-driven formula of earlier decades

- the use of technology, the effect of the multiplexes and niche marketing

- the significant contribution of diasporic Indian filmmakers, particularly from Canada, the USA and the UK, as well as substantial contributions to music.

In the decade up to 2004, Bollywood produced four of its biggest commercial hits – *Hum Aapke Hain Koun!; Dilwale Dulhania Le Jayenge; Gadar – Ek Prem Katha* and *Koi Mil Gaya* (I've Found Someone, 2003). Two were directed by young debutants belonging to established filmmaking families, while *Gadar – Ek Prem Katha* was conceived and produced by a leading television channel, Zee Telefilms, entirely on corporate lines. We discuss this film in some detail further on.

The advent of a fresh breed of directors eager to upgrade the time-honoured Bollywood mould and the process of corporatisation of film production were both indicative of the shape of things to come. *Koi Mil Gaya*, a successful marriage of a Hollywood-inspired storyline and tried-and-tested Bollywood ingredients, was produced by Rakesh Roshan. But it was his son, Hrithik, who catapulted to fame with *Kaho Naa Pyaar Hai* (Say You Love Me, 2000).

The Changing Star System

The partial eclipse of films linked with Amitabh Bachchan is illustrative of the shift in the star system. He grappled for some years with mounting debts, constant flops and few roles worthy of his talent and skills. His attempt to make a long-awaited comeback with *Mrityudaata* (Death-Giver, 1997) was an unmitigated disaster. He failed miserably in a string of films that followed: *Major Saab* (The Major, 1998); *Lal Badshah* (Red Emperor, 1998); *Hindustan Ki Kasam* (In the Name of India, 1999); *Kohraam* (The Great Clash, 1999) and *Suryvansham* (The Clash of the Sun, 1999).

But Amitabh Bachchan became television's hottest property overnight as the host of the successful quiz show on Star Plus, *Kaum Banega Crorepati* (Who Wants to be a Millionaire? 2000). Since then, he has reinvented himself on the big screen by playing his age in Aditya Chopra's second film, *Mohabbatein* (Varieties of Love, 2000). The Indian clone of Who Wants to be a Millionaire? quickly redefined the parameters of prime-time entertainment and his cinematic career blossomed anew. He has been cast as a father figure in several films: *Ek Ristha* (A Bond of Love, 2001); *Armaan* (2003) and *Baghban* (The Gardener, 2003). Though none was a commercial success, his towering screen presence and his undoubted acting skills have emphasised his status as a mega star.

Despite Hrithik Roshan's dramatic rise to stardom he did not do too well at the box office with his later releases; *Mission Kashmir* (2000); *Yadein* (Memories, 2001); *Fiza* (2001); *Aap Mujhe Achehe Lagne Lage* (I am Falling in Love, 2002) and *Naa Tum Jaano Naa Hum* (Neither You Know Nor I, 2002). In 2003 the combination of father Rakesh Roshan and son, Hrithik delivered the successful *Koi Mil Gaya*, a sci-fi drama inspired by Steven Spielberg's ET. This hugely entertaining film has the star playing an adult trapped in the body of an 11-year-old. His life changes forever when he chances upon an alien stranded on earth and befriends the strange creature.

It is unlikely that the handsome Hrithik will be the next real superstar of the Indian screen. The concept of a one-man industry, of an overarching superstar who could hold the giant Mumbai dream machine together, died with the temporary eclipse of Bachchan in the early 1990s. By the mid-1990s, the vacuum was filled by a whole new group of male stars, led by the Khan triumvirate (Shahrukh, Aamir and Salman), who together now shoulder the burden of keeping the industry in good health. As production costs escalated and expensive films featuring the biggest stars of the day collapsed at the box office, the inescapable truth hit home: the sheer enormity of the commercial clout that Bachchan enjoyed in the preceding decades would be difficult to match, let alone surpass.

Of the three Khans, it is Sharukh Khan who has moved to the top of the Bollywood male stars league, with successful films such as *Karan Arjun* (Karan and Arjun, 1995); *Dilwale Dulhania Le Jayenge*; *Dil To Pagal Hai* and *Kuch Kuch Hota Hai*. He has set up his own production company, Dreamz Unlimited and, after a rather difficult start, has been successful with *Chalte Chalte* (The Course of Life, 2003), an entertaining tale of a young couple grappling with marital discord, starring himself and Rani Mukerjee and directed by Aziz Mirza.

Salman Khan is a dashing young man and, although some doubt has been expressed about his acting skills, he has starred in successful films such as *Karan Arjun; Hum Dil De Chuke Sanam* (I Am in Love, 1999) and *Biwi No.1* (Wife Number 1, 1999).

Aamir Khan has enviable status as a craftsman and a diligent actor. He is reckoned as a safe box office bet ever since in his debut in Mansoor Khan's *Qayamat Se Qayamat Tak* (Love is Forever, 1988); *Dil Chahta Hai* (My Heart's Desire, 2001) and *Lagaan*, which is discussed below.

Of the female stars, Madhuri Dixit gave mass hysteria new meaning, achieving near-cult status in such films as *Tezaab* (Acid, 1988); *Ram Lakhan* (1989); *Dil* (1990); *Hum Aapke Hain Koun?* (1994); *Raja* (1995) and *Dil To Pagal Hai.* Her recent films – *Wajood* (Identity, 1999); *Pukaar* (The Cry, 2000) and *Gaya Gamini* (The Elephant's Gait, 2000) – all flopped and her return to the film industry after her marriage, in *Yeh Raaste Hain Pyaar Ke* (Such are the Ways of Love, 2001), was uninspiring. Her brief but sparkling appearance in the multistar cast *Lajja* (Shame, 2001) proved what was already well known – that Madhuri Dixit has no peer in the business and that even if the hits were to stop flowing, her natural talent will not.

Meanwhile, younger stars such as Kajol, Karisma Kapoor, Kareena Kapoor and Aishwarya Rai have taken over from Madhuri Dixit and lead the box-office chase.

The New Patriot

Many of the films listed early in this chapter were aimed at whipping up nationalist sentiments as Hindu nationalism rose. The earlier films dealt with nationalist and patriotic themes, but the recent ones tend mostly to be about bashing Pakistan. According to Jha (2001: 1-3), it was J.P. Dutta's *Border* (1997) that named the enemy for the first time. Some of these have already been discussed, such as *Roja* (see p40-41) and *Bombay* (p68). *Gadar – Ek Prem Katha* weaved violence with a jingoistic love story around the cataclysmic events that were sparked off by the partition of India. The film tells of a Sikh truck driver who falls in love with a Muslim girl amid the chaos of Partition in 1947 and who takes on the might of the 'enemy nation' to wrest his Muslim wife back from her family. This highly entertaining film with its superb performances by Sunny Deol and Amisha Patel led the film's director, Anil Sharma and lead actor Sunny Deol to repeat the formula in *The Hero* (2003). This was the story of an intrepid Indian spy who outwits a bunch of 'evil' Pakistanis bent upon acquiring a nuclear device. But this time, the expensive thriller failed commercially, despite its anti-Pakistan slant.

Also asserting nationhood is *Lagaan* (2001), directed by Gowariker, but this film is in a different class. Much has been written about the impact of *Lagaan* on the Indian and world audience since it received an American Academy Award nomination in the Best Foreign Film category (see Majumdar, 2001;

Mannathukkaren, 2001; Nagy, 2002 and Chakraborty, 2003). The story re-volves around a group of villagers in 1893 playing cricket in Champaner in Kutch against an oppressive colonial regime to save their lives. An ideal blending of two hugely popular Indian pastimes – cricket and popular cinema – *Lagaan* is a polysemic text. Majumdar (2001: abstract) along with others, views the film as 'evidence of Indian resistance to British imperialism as well as a commentary on the evolution and development of cricket in colonial India'.

Mannathukkaren (2001) finds some of Majumdar's suggestions rather exaggerated and challenges the claim that

> *Lagaan* captures the pulse of the Indian nation state [and is] a nationalist tale depicted via the fortunes of the country's most popular game. (p4581)

Mannathukkaren concedes that theoretically, Majumdar's thesis that the 'domain of leisure can be appropriated as a means of resistance against the colonial regime holds good'. But he contends that 'for structural reasons, the kind of patronage, the communal structure of cricket organisation and lack of a mass base, it did not become so until the 1930s'(2001: 4583).

Other commentators such as Nagy (2002) argue that the film, particularly the subtitle 'Once Upon a Time in India' can be read mythologically, asserting that 'The god worshipped by the Hindu villagers and whose cult is explained to the inquiring Elizabeth, is Krishna' (p295).

Superbly scripted, peopled by believable characters, and transmitting genuinely positive messages, *Lagaan* quickly achieved cult status. It reminded sceptics of the power Hindi popular films are capable of exercising over the masses without sacrificing quality. Deservedly, *Lagaan* is already being talked of as a film in the exalted league of *Mother India* (1957), *Mughal-e-Azam* (The Great Mughal, 1960) and *Sholay* (1975).

Notably, the commercial success of *Gadar – Ek Prem Katha* triggered the revival of interest in films about true or fictionalised incidents and person-ages from history. The best known of these films is the life and times of the legendary freedom fighter Shaheed Bhagat Singh (2002), starring Ajay Devgan. Ajay Devgan started his career as an action star but has developed into a strong dramatic actor and has a brooding presence on screen. He won a National Award as Best Actor for his performance in *Zakhm* (Wound, 1998) and in 2002 was similarly honoured for his role as Bhagat Singh. His perfor-mance as an upright policeman in *Gangaajal* (Water of the Ganges, 2003) has also been highly praised.

As this book goes to press, India can expect the release of a string of war films centred on the Indo-Pak Kargil conflict of the late 1990s. Among them are Farhan Akhtar's *Lakshya* (Bull's Eye), scripted by his father and famous poet-lyricist Javed Akhtar, and *LOC: Kargil* (Line of Control) made by J.P. Dutta. Popular patriotism, it seems, is still a viable commercial proposition.

Designer Films

Hits such as *Hum Aapke Hain Koun!; Dilwale Dulhania Le Jayenge*; and *Kuch Kuch Hota Hai* are carefully packaged and branded. Every visual and physical detail, from the components that make up the backdrop to the attire and accessories of the stars, looks more like a lifestyle and fashion statement than an intrinsic part of the story. Fashion designers such as Mahesh Malhotra and choreographers such as Farah Khan have a crucial input to such films. The emphasis on food (in *Hum Aapke Hain Koun!*), sleek cars (in *Dilwale Dulhania Le Jayenge*) and body-hugging costumes (in *Kuch Kuch Hota Hai*) deliberately emphasise the ideology of consumption (see Chatterjee, in Gulzar *et al* (2003: chapter 7) for an insightful discussion).

Satellite channels such as ZeeTV and Star have undoubtedly created the conditions for consumerism. The characters in some of the soap operas televised on ZeeTV live 'in beautiful bungalows with expensive furniture and at any time of the day women wear heavy make up and designer clothes' (Gokulsing, 2004).

With Farhan Akhtar's remarkably fresh *Dil Chahta Hai*, the designer film acquired a soul of its own. It features rich young urban characters. Its three love stories are about real people with tangible emotions. It depicts the 'global Indian' who wears imported clothing, flies to foreign lands at will, drives executive foreign cars and sports a designer haircut. He exists in the film not merely to attract the diasporic and urban Indian audience but also to signal the problems that confront 'India's Generation Now'. He is an Indian who is still rooted in the values of the land but is unapologetic about embracing the material trappings of affluence and western influence.

No film has captured the audience's obsession with glitz better than Sanjay Leela Bhansali's *Devdas* (2002). It is a grandiloquent retelling of a tragic love story filmed twice before. In 1935 K.L. Saigal played the legendary self-destructive Devdas, directed by P.C. Barua, and Dilip Kumar starred in the 1955 version by Bimal Roy. In the 2002 remake by Bhansali, the star is Sharukh Khan and thus *Devdas* has little in common with the style of the earlier two films. It is meant for the post-MTV generation; it is loud, melodramatic, ornate and laced with elaborate musical set pieces. Bhansali employs conventions from opera and traditional Indian theatre forms such as *nautanki, jatra* and *Raslila* to pare the tragic tinge from the tale of doomed love and proffer instead what looks like a celebration of life in the face of tragic destiny.

Hit Combinations

One of the most talked about box office phenomena of the 1990s was the consistent popularity of the prolific partnership of David Dhawan and Govinda. It yielded a series of successful hits beginning with *Aankhen* (Eyes, 1993) and stretching to *Hero No.1* (1997). By the end of the decade, however, the Dhawan formula had begun to wear thin: even Govinda's spontaneity could not save *Kunwara* (2000). In 2001, the partnership was back in business with *Jodi No.1,* but not for long. There were few takers for Govinda's brand of comedy and Dhawan, too, seemed to have lost his golden touch. Two of his latest releases, *Hum Kisise Kum Nahin* (We are Second to None, 2002), starring Amitabh Bachchan, Ajay Devgan and Aishwarya Rai, and *Ek Aur Ek Gyarah* (One Plus One Equals Eleven) starring Sanjay Dutt and Govinda, did not fare well at the box office.

Diasporic Indian Filmmakers

We have shown that diasporic Indian filmmaking in the United Kingdom has a long history – forty five years ago, Ismail Merchant blazed the trail with *How the West was Won.* From the 1960s a string of films has been produced by the Merchant-Ivory-Jhabvala partnership, including *The Householder* (1963); *Shakespeare Wallah* (1965); *The Guru* (1969); *Bombay Talkie* (1970); *Heat and Dust* (1983) (see the latest edition of *The Films of Merchant Ivory* by Long).

Of Hanif Kureishi's writings, *My Beautiful Laundrette* (1985) and *The Buddha of Suburbia* (1991) are two significant contributions to diasporic Indian filmmaking. In *The Buddha of Suburbia* his character Karim is a blend of Englishness and Indianness. Kureishi manages to capture the kind of identity crisis which informs the films of Chadha and Nair who, together with Metha, have illuminated diasporic Indian filmmaking.

In the UK, the wave of immigrants who came mainly from the Commonwealth during the 1950s, '60s and '70s encountered much racism. However, while organisations and academics were struggling to redraw the map of multicultural Britain (Parekh, 2002; Modood *et al.*, 1997; Gilroy, 1991; The Commission for Racial Equality) the children and grandchildren of the first wave of immigrants have asserted themselves in all aspects of life in the United Kingdom. And while questions about Indianness, Asianness, Blackness and Britishness in multicultural Britain are now part of a larger debate about diaspora in contemporary discussions of migration and identity (see Braziel and Mannur, 2003 for example), the 1990s saw the following developments.

From Canada, Deepa Metha's *Fire* (1998) has proved controversial. It depicts the relationship between two brides, sisters-in-law, in the North Indian urban home of a middle class extended family. In the words of Gopinath (2003: 271):

> Filmmaker Deepa Metha quickly establishes the familiar familial violences and confusions that underlie this space of home: both women (ironically named Radha and Sita) do most of the labor for the family business while their husbands alternately abuse or ignore them; this eventually precipitates them turning to each other for sex and emotional sustenance.

This treatment of women by unfeeling men is an essential element of Metha's film. What she is trying to do is hold up the mirror of social change in contemporary India, but the film did not go down as well as expected. It was seen as a feminist tract, particularly in its portrayal of all men in the story as 'boorish, perverted, or good old-fashioned male chauvinist pigs while the women are downtrodden and victimized' (Unterberger, 1999: 234).

Fire (1996) was scheduled as the first of a trilogy; *Earth* appeared in 1999. At the time of writing, the filming of *Water* has been held up, as Metha's attempt to shoot it in the holy city of Varanasi in India met with fierce protest from Hindu nationalists and she had to stop work on it.

Mira Nair's astounding success as a diasporic filmmaker in the USA is due to a number of factors. Born in Orissa, India, she went to the Irish Catholic School of Simla, then studied at the Universities of Delhi and Harvard (USA). She also spent time in Africa as a filmmaker. These experiences had a formative impact on her life and career. As she says, she coped well with home, displacement, nomadism since 'a brown person, between black and white, I could move between these worlds very comfortably because I was neither'(Tasker, 2002:264).

Her films aim to draw on her experiences 'to provoke, challenge and rupture the borders of identities on class, race, gender and location' (Tasker, 2002: 363). In one of her early films, *So Far from India*, Nair depicts the grim realities facing Ashok, an Indian immigrant to New York seeking a better paid job to support his pregnant wife whom he has left behind in India. The film, uses qualities of *cinéma-vérité** to record 'the duality of the immigrant reality, the slow disintegration of rootedness, the new avenues and road-blocks of assimilation and belonging' (Shah, 1987: 22-24).

Salaam Bombay (1988), winner of the New Director's Award at Cannes and an Oscar Nomination in 1989, clearly shows Nair's preoccupations with those who are marginalised in society. Again using elements of *cinéma-vérité*, she tells the story of Chaipu, a young boy who goes to Bombay to make some money. The world he moves in is peopled with prostitutes and drug addicts.

> His gaze demands a multiplicity of viewing positions and [Nair] re-peatedly cross-identifies him with oppressed women (prostitutes and children) through eye matches and gazes that lead the viewer (whether from New York, Bombay or London) to involve themselves in the embodied subjectivities of fictional constructs. (Tasker, 2002:266)

Nair's next film *Mississippi Masala* (1991) is ostensibly a love story about a young Indian woman (Mina, played by Sarita Choudhury) and a young black man (Demetrius, played by Denzel Washington). The film presents 'a narrative of exiled Indian people who were forced out of Uganda under the regime of Idi Amin' (Tasker, 2002:267), and features issues found in Nair's earlier films and documentaries: exile, difference and border crossings of African and Asian diasporic communities.

Kama Sutra (1996) received far less praise than *Salaam Bombay* or *Mississippi Masala*. Set in 16th Century India, the film subverts the well-known book of love by having a servant girl seduce the King, the husband of the princess with whom the girl grew up. Although the film is beautifully crafted, it was generally criticised for its lack of passionate intensity. Nair could not get the film screened in India because scenes showing kissing were still prohibited there. With *Monsoon Wedding* (2002), Nair returned to the lime-light, winning the Golden Lion award at the 2001 Venice International Film Festival. The film is a joyous, colourful celebration of a Punjabi wedding and chronicles the events leading up to a last minute arranged marriage in upper middle-class Delhi. In the words of Macnab (2002: 19):

> Tradition and modernity clash headlong, secrets are revealed, romances blossom. Dhawan's screenplay has two focal points: the negotiations be-tween the would-be bride and groom (and)... the spontaneous romance that springs up between Dubey, the cellphone-wielding event manager organising the wedding, and the family's sweet-natured maid Alice.

---

* *Cinéma-vérité* – A simplistic definition of this concept is that it tries to catch reality on film. It is unstaged, non-dramatised, non-narrative cinema (see Hayward, 2000: 58-59)

In an interview after winning the award, Nair acknowledged that the film is partly autobiographical:

> While *Monsoon Wedding* is a portrait of modern contemporary India, it is also a very personal story about my kind of people, Punjabi people. It is a community that works hard, parties hard and has a huge appetite for life. (*Filmmaker*, 2002:78)

The successes achieved by Nair in the USA are largely paralleled by those of Gurinder Chadha in the UK. Her *Bhaji on the Beach* (1993) is about a group of Punjabi Indian women who come together for a day trip to Blackpool in the north of England. The characters span the generations, from teenage girls to a grandmother figure and

> the film seems to suggest that this generation of diaspora is not only different from the generation before or the generation being constituted in another site, it is also different *within*. (Shukla, 2003: 237)

The characters in *Bhaji on the Beach* connect with the debate on Indianness, Britishness and multiculturalism. The characters have multiple identities: Indian, Asian, Black and British.

It is her *Bend it like Beckham* (2002) which has won Chadha international acclaim. This comedy drama is about two girls trying to break into the male-dominated world of football. The film builds on the UK's fascination with football and the skills of player David Beckham, then at Manchester United, who has attained iconic status. *Bend it like Beckham* follows the progress of an Indian girl, played by Parminder Nagra, who 'idolises Beckham and a white English girl who idolises US woman football legend Mia Hamm (a canny move for the US market) and their battles to play the game' (*Screen International*, 2001:13). Chadha focused on the girls and their family lives. Her choice of title signals that the film was as much about bending society's rules as bending a ball *à la* Beckham.

A new film produced by Puneet Sira, a London-born director, takes the social commentary on Britain much further, making it the subject of his film. Consequently, *I...Proud to be an Indian* is quite different from the films of other diasporic filmmakers. Based on the director's experiences of growing up in East London in the 1970s, the style draws more on the work of artistic filmmakers such as Adoor Gopalakrishnan, Shyam Benegal and Mani Kaul, among others (see p34) though it was made on a budget of £600,000. It was shot in London by a mixed crew of Indians and Britons.

What Sira does is to puncture the fantasy world of Bollywood films that romanticise the British background and instead give Indians in India some idea of the racism and violence faced by Indian immigrants to Britain in the 1970s. He believes that the vast majority of people in India do not know what the BNP stands for, for example. He is reported to have said: 'This film will make Indians understand that all is not good in the West. There is a dark side to Western society too.'

There are few singing and dancing routines but the film does conform to the Bollywood formula of action and melodrama. Sira is aiming to appeal to audiences in India and elsewhere. *I...Proud to be an Indian* is an interesting departure from the recent string of films about bashing Pakistanis, particularly as Indian films are watched by Pakistanis who are settled outside the sub-continent, in, for example, the Middle East.

The rivalry in Britain between Indian and Pakistani immigrants is also explored in the film, and this could prove controversial in India The hero, played by Bollywood actor Shail Kumar Singh, is an Indian immigrant whose middle-class family endures racist attacks before finally deciding to take revenge. He sinks his differences with a Pakistani to fight back against skinhead thugs and the pair become close friends.

Sira moved from London to Mumbai in 1998 to run their trendy music channel, Channel 5. 'There is plenty of blood' Sira said about his film, but he denied that it was anti-British. He told *The Times*:

> I hope it will open the eyes of Indians to the problems of violence if they visit [Britain], but it's not all negative. We have made sure we included a sympathetic police character, called Sergeant Barnes, who tries to help victims of racism. (Nick Meo, *The Times* 12 December 2003)

Fusion and Fission

Another of the contributions of diasporic Indians currently enjoying universal popularity is their music. In *Mississippi Masala* (1991) Nair's appeal to black spectators is enhanced by a soundtrack that is a mélange of African, Indian, African-American and worldbeat music.

Music is of course what endears the Indian spectators to their cinema. In this regard, the role of the playback singers – Lata Mangeshkar, Asha Bhonsle, Anurada Padwal, Alka Yagnik, Manna Day, Sonu Nigam and the late legendary Mukesh, Talat Mahmood, Mohammad Rafi, Kishore Kumar among others – is crucial. Few Indian films can succeed without a generous dose of popular music. In recent years, bhangra music has become hugely popular. As Dudrah (2002) observes:

> British bhangra is a genre of British popular music fusing Punjabi lyrics and the beats of the Indian drum, the dhol, with black music genres and

British pop sounds, producing an urban anthem and commentary about the lives of its British South Asian audience. (*Abstract*: 363)

Bhangra lyrics are sung 'primarily in Punjabi, a regional language spoken in the states of Punjab in both India and Pakistan'. Not all British Asians speak or understand Punjabi, but nevertheless

> the wider appeal of British bhangra is due to the fact that it is an energetic fusion-based dance music that can be enjoyed by a number of different British Asians other than Punjabis. (Dudrah, 2002: 381)

A number of bands – Achanak, Apna Group, Safri Boyz *inter alia* – have flourished, particularly in Birmingham, and artistes such as Apache Indian and Bally Sagoo are more widely marketable (see Sharma *et al.*, 1996).

Critical Reflections on Diasporic Indian Filmmakers

The term diaspora is derived from the Greek 'to disperse' and is most usually applied to the dispersal of the Jews. Over time, however, many people have undergone sustained dispersions and the term diaspora is now applied to ethnic groups such as African-Americans in the USA, African-Caribbeans in the UK (see Gilroy, 1993; Mercer, 1994, among others) and South Asians in the UK (Brah, 1996 and Shukla, 2003 among others).

Theoretically speaking, we can locate the contributions of disaporic Indian filmmakers within the postcolonial tradition. Postcolonialism is about resistance to colonialism and imperialism. It seeks

> to analyse the global effects of European condition... Edward Said's (1978) *Orientalism* is widely regarded as one of the founding texts of postcolonial theory. (Macey, 2000: 304)

There is a substantial body of literature on postcolonialism/postcolonial theory (see *inter alia* Spivak, 1987; Mishra and Hodge, 1991; Williams and Chrisman, 1994, Ashcroft *et al.*, 1995; and Young, 2001). Shukla (2003: 16) asserts that:

> to call the Indian diasporas of the post-1947 period 'postcolonial' [then] signifies a great deal more than chronology... underscoring relationships to British rule frames the cultures of Indians abroad historically and also embeds them in a global framework.

The New Face of the Indian Film Industry

By the end of the 1990s, the Mumbai film industry was on the threshold of a welcome new dawn. The government had granted industry status to filmmaking, nationalised banks were showing some interest in funding professionally handled, time-bound projects, and a few big ventures even received insurance cover. By 2003, several blue-chip corporate houses entered the film production sector. These included Applause Entertainment, floated by Kumaramangalam Birla of the Aditya Birla Group, Cutting Edge Entertainment, a subsidiary of Tata Infomedia, Crossover Films and Galaxy Entertainment Corporation, both promoted by NRI investor Purnendu Chatterjee. Also during 2003, the Hinduja Group's In Network was actively involved in the production of Hindi films. As a result, the haphazard, star-driven style of production began to give way to boardroom confabulations, bound scripts, structured shooting schedules and institutional funding. The industry began to wear a more organised look than ever before.

Several Hollywood studios that had engaged only in the distribution of foreign cinematic imports now began acquiring the marketing rights of locally produced Hindi films as well. Twentieth Century Fox joined hands with leading Mumbai producer-director Ram Gopal Varma to produce Hindi films, and also acquired films as diverse as the romantic comedy, *Jhan Kaar Beats* and *Pinjar* (Skeleton), a Partition era drama based on a Punjabi literary masterpiece, for commercial distribution during 2003.

The Ram Gopal Varma Factory

In the new millennium, Varma went from strength to strength as he rapidly built on his well-deserved reputation as a filmmaker who believed in the virtues of experimentation. He followed up *Satya* with another stylised underworld drama, *Company*. In 2003, he directed *Bhoot* (Ghost), a revisionist horror film that relocates the customary haunted house in a high rise apartment block in the heart of metropolitan Mumbai. Both films achieved cult status even as they rewrote narrative rules. Equally significantly, Varma continued his policy of raising aspiring filmmakers from complete obscurity and catapulting them into the thick of the action. Many of his one-time assistants and technicians – E.Niwas, Rajah Mukherjee, Chandan Arora, Prawaal Raman, among others – are today established directors.

These directors brought a radically new sensibility to the film industry. E. Niwas and Rajah Mukherjee crafted gripping films that adopted established popular Hindi cinema conventions to tell disturbing and unusually realistic stories. In *Shool* (Thorns, 2000), Niwas focused on an upright, intrepid policeman in a small Bihar town where politics and venality are synonymous, while in *Pyaar Tune Kya Kiya* (The Ways of Love, 2001), Mukherjee drew a convincing portrait of a temperamental woman who is obsessed with a married man.

Further developments in the Indian industry include the increasing use of new technology, accounting for multiplex cinemas. This, together with the potential of VCD and DVD rights and a growing demand for satellite broadcasting, has changed the economics of the film business, opening up several revenue-earning avenues and a rapidly expanding overseas market.

The Indian Cinema Audience

While there is a substantial literature on audience studies for television, there is comparatively little on the audience for Indian cinema. And there is virtually nothing about their behaviour during the showing of a film. Srinivas (2002) has made some insightful comments on the culture of reception that is so distinctive to Indian cinema. Steve Derné's (Derné and Jadwin, 2000) study of the ethnography of men's filmgoing in India enables us to examine Mulvey's (1975) contention that film-viewing technologies contribute to the power of the male gaze. Indian popular cinema, as we have shown, has a broad appeal that is based on a mix of ingredients (masala) that include comic elements, romantic themes, family drama, song and dance sequences. There is something for everyone.

> Movie experiences in India involve families, friends and co-workers. Groups may be composed of four to eight, even ten individuals or more. Families include all ages – even infants are brought to the theatre and toddlers and the elderly are part of the group... (Srinivas, 2002: 160)

Women rarely go to the cinema by themselves. What is remarkable is the behaviour of men, who may walk out of the cinema hall during the performance, choosing appropriate moments to come back in so as not to miss a song and dance sequence, for example. Some spectators are 'repeaters', who see the same film – or parts of it— time and time again.

Another noticeable difference between Indian spectators and those in the West is that watching a film is an interactive/participatory experience. Some spectators, generally men and usually those in the inexpensive seats near the screen, comment on the parts of the story that make them uncomfortable and whistle or clap if they particularly approve of a scene.

Laura Mulvey (1975/1989) has asserted that the cinema contributes to male power by enabling men to make women the objects of a controlling gaze – which she identified as scopophilia. 'Using another person as an object of sexual stimulation through sight is one of the primary pleasures of the cinema' (Derné and Jadwin, 2000: 244). Although Mulvey has subsequently recognised that films also position women filmgoers to gaze at on-screen images, it is true that women are objectified in the cinema, as for example in *Bandit Queen*.

Derné and Jadwin (2000) demonstrate that the clear-cut distinction between the men who are looking and the women being watched is not a universal feature of male dominance. In their ethnographic study of male filmgoers in India, they found that many men are attracted to the heroine's modesty – their favourites being Madhuri Dixit, Sridevi, Judi Chawla *inter alia* – who all have a reputation for modest dress and behaviour.

But it is true also that men gaze not only at women but also at men. Drawing our attention to William Holden's bodily displays in *Picnic* (1954), Derné and Jadwin (2000) observe that, according to Cohen, cinema has always invested in the spectacle of the male body. In Hindi films such displays are enjoyed by both male and female audiences – fan magazines and the Indian press often comment on male actors' bodies – for example, Salman Khan often makes a point of showing off his sculptured body. Closeness between male stars, as in *Sholay* (see Dissanayake and Sahai, 1992: 95), is sometimes seen as having a homoerotic component. Jani, a female journalist, writing about Indian cinema, describes 'how the camera focuses on Jackie Shroff's groin as he dances suggestively 'thrusting his pelvis back and forth'' (quoted in Derné and Jadwin, 2000: 261).

Sex scenes and the censors' dilemma
The absurd double standards operated by the Central Board of Film Certificate (CBFC) are well known. On the one hand, 'lascivious, lewd song and dance sequences and gratuitous violence routinely escape the censors' scissors, and Hollywood offerings with torrid sex scenes get the Universal or U rating' (*India Today*, 2002: editorial). On the other hand, kissing and artistically erotic scenes are cut by the CBFC. Consequently, a number of filmmakers such as Adoor Gopala Krishnan, Ram Gopal Varma, Mahesh Bhatt and Mira Nair have been victims of the whims of the CBFC. Adoor Gopalakrishnan regards the CBFC as incongruous in a modern democracy. And Ram Gopal Varma points out that the upper classes can see whatever they want on DVD and video, anyway. Mahesh Bhatt maintains that pornographic films should be legitimised; his *Raaz* (2202) had some nude scenes cut and expletives deleted by the CBFC. It cost Mira Nair about £40,000 to recut *Kama Sutra: A Tale of Love* and her *Monsoon Wedding* also suffered from the scissors of the CBFC.

In 2002, the controversy surrounding the screening of sexually explicit films came to a head. In an attempt to eliminate the confusion created by the

Bandit Queen

CBFC's lack of clear criteria and the myopic view of the process of film-making in a globalised India, Vijay Anand, then the Chair of the CBFC, sub-mitted the following proposals to the government:

• No more censoring of films. Instead give ratings like U, U/A and A and enforce them strictly.

• Have a M/A (mature adult) category for sexually explicit films, to be shown in special theatres.

• Free the CBFC from the clutches of the Information and Broadcasting Ministry. Also guarantee fiscal autonomy.

• Ensure half the board members of the CBFC are aged 20 to 30, as 75 per cent of audience are youth.

• Films shown on TV should also be brought under the ambit of the board to end dual standards. (*India Today*, 2002: 45)

The government was unwilling to accept these radical proposals, particularly the establishment of separate theatres for pornographic films. Vijay Anand resigned as Chair of the CBFC in July 2002. In an interview with *India Today* (2002: 48) he criticised the CBFC for appointing members

... who were shopkeepers yesterday passing judgements on cinema as CBFC members today.

They don't look at a film in its entirety – they are just looking to suggest cuts. We wanted members to have a film background so that they under-stood the process of filmmaking.

The Ministry of Information and Broadcasting argued that all over the world governments were fighting against pornography.

The new Chair of the CBFC, BJP MP Arvind Trivedi Lankesh (who played Ravana in the serial *Ramayan* telecast on Doordarshan in the 1980s) says he firmly believes in upholding the Indian culture in all its purity. He is reported to have said 'Films are our *Gangotri**, don't soil them' (*The Times of India* Special Report, 28 July 2002).

Yet the screening of pornographic films is big business in the Malayalam and Tamil industries. Of the 90 or so films released in 2001 by the Malayalam industry, at least one-third celebrated the statuesque charms of porn stars such as Shakeela.

* *Gangotri* is the source of the river Ganges in the Attimalayas. It denotes purity – the river Ganges/Ganga becomes progressively more polluted as it flows down the mountains, through the plains, all the way to the Bay of Bengal.

In the words of Prasannarajan (2002: 51)

... The so-called Shakeela wave that swept away the Malayalees to the heaving, panting, swooning dark halls of sexual salvation. It was all about heavy-breathing men with Saddam moustaches struggling with their hands and faces on thunder thighs. Culturally, it is a historic moment in the life of the so-called progressive Kerala. After communism, pornography has become the liberation theology of the working class... (For further details see *India Today* – Is Sex OK? 5 August, 2002.)

CHAPTER 8

Regional Cinemas of India

Regional cinemas are the key to the Indian cinema industry. India is unique in its kaleidoscope of diverse languages and cultures: there are at least 15 languages and over 2000 dialects, and films are produced in most of the official languages. In 1993, for example, 183 films were made in Hindi, 168 in Tamil and 148 in Telugu. The largest number of films are produced in these three languages. However, 78 films were made in Kannada, 71 in Malayalam, 57 in Bengali, 35 in Marathi and almost 10 in Assamese.

This book's emphasis on the Bombay cinema is justifiable in that it represents Hindi-speaking films and is indeed synonymous with Indian popular cinema. Although we can talk of regional cinemas, there is an incessant cross-over of talents – Bengali film directors direct Hindi or Oriya films; Tamil directors direct Telugu films. Actors and actresses from the South play leading roles in films made in the North. Furthermore, some of the well-known figures in Indian cinema, particularly in the artistic tradition, come from the regional cinemas. The diverse regional cinemas in India strive to maintain their distinctive identities and provide an important dimension of the cultural wealth and diversity of India's regional cinemas.

One of the smallest film-producing regions, Assam, is in the extreme north east of India and its 20 million inhabitants speak Assamese and Bengali. The region is little known to the rest of India because of its remoteness. It is neglected; it depends heavily on agriculture and the only industries are tea and oil. According to Mazid (1996), such conditions were unfavourable to the birth of cinema, because filmmaking is an industrial activity.

Assam did not produce any silent films. Its first film, *Joymoti*, was produced in 1935 by Agarwalla, who drew on historical and literary sources to depict the tragic patriotism of a princess, while also portraying 'parallels with the situation of disorder and disharmony unleashed by the British rule on the people of Assam for aligning themselves with the National Movement' (Mazid, 1996:53). Although not a commercial success, it is notable that at a time when the Bombay cinema was producing mythological films, *Joymoti* was about an historical event.

A number of films (*Badan Barphukan*, 1948; *Lachit Barphukan*, 1960; *Maniram Dewan*, 1963) made from the 1940s to the 1960s were about personalities who sacrificed their lives for the cause of the Indian Freedom Movement. In 1964 Hazarika's *Pratidhwani* (The Echo) won him the President's Silver medal for the best film in Assamese. Based on a popular legend of the Khasi people, it 'tells the story of a poor shepherd boy and his love for a girl whom the hill King takes as his concubine. The film ends tragically with the shepherd boy being burnt alive' (Garga 1996:305).

The films produced since the 1970s include *Bristi* (Deluge, 1974), *Sandhyaraag* (Evening Song, 1977), *Sankalpat* (Line of Conviction, 1986), *Juge Juge Sangram* (Decades of Struggle, 1986) and *Sutrapat* (The Beginning, 1987). Most are about village life versus city life (*Sandhyaraag*) or about the Assam agitation which took place between 1979 and 1985. Both *Sankalpat* and *Juge Juge Sangram* are about justice for the Assamese people and the causes of the agitation.

Land disputes in rural Assam (*Halodhia Choraya Baodhan Khai*, The Catastrophe, 1978) and environmental concerns (*Banani*, Forest, 1989) are of considerable concern to the Assamese. Some of the films make only oblique references to the political issues. However, Gogoi's *Surya Tejor Anya Naam* (Sun is the Other Name of Blood) launched in 1991, is about the cause of independent Assam. Whether overt politics will become significant in Assamese cinema remains to be seen.

Jahnu Barua is one of Assam's best-known directors and has produced a number of remarkable films – *Aparoop* (1982), *Papoori* (1986), *Hkhagaroloi Boho Door* (It is a Long Way to the Sea, 1994). His *Haldhia Choraya Baodhan Khai* (already mentioned) won the Golden Lotus in India in 1988 and the Grand Prix for best film and best actor at Locarno (Garga 1996:307).

Kannada Cinema

Located in the state of Karnataka with over 40 million people and 1200 cinema halls (in 1993), Kannada cinema was to a large extent under the shadow of the neighbouring Tamil and Telugu film industries for a long time. Unlike Assamese cinema, the vast majority of the films produced in Kannada are of the popular variety – sentimental, melodramatic, escapist, full of songs and dance. However, a few filmmakers are keen to create a serious cinema that addresses significant social issues.

Mohan Bhavanami, the Chief Producer of the Film Division of the Government of India, made the first Kannada silent film, *Mricchakatika*, in 1929. In 1932 came two talkies, *Bhaktha Dhruva* and *Sati Sulochana*. At first the theatre provided the inspiration and artistic resources for the filmmakers, but cinema evolved somewhat sporadically until the 1950s. There were several reasons for this: the absence of entrepreneurship, lack of adequate technical facilities and the contentment of the audiences with seeing Hindi, Tamil and Telugu films. However, by the 1960s, the State Government decided to introduce subsidies for film production and to recognise good filmmaking by instituting an award system.

Samskara (Funeral Rites, 1970) by Telugu poet Pattabhi Rama Reddy has been discussed. A number of highly talented filmmakers followed Reddy: B.V. Karanth, Girish Karnad, G.V. Iyer and Girish Kasaravalli deserve special mention. Karanth's *Chomanadudi* (Chomana's Drum, 1975) highlights the strengths of the artistic cinema in Karnataka. Set in the 1930s, it concerns an old man, Chomana, who is filled with rage and despair over the poverty and social injustices he has daily to encounter. Only by playing his drum can he give expression to his pent-up feelings. He is perturbed by the humiliations that his children have to put up with. He dies an unhappy man, but the sound of his drum continues to arouse his fellow citizens.

Two years earlier, Girish Karnad made *Kaddu* (The Forest, 1973), set in the past and exploring the nature of violence that characterised feudal societies. Garga (1996: 281) remarked that 'The analysis of the socio-economic causes of feudal violence and decay is enriched by minutely observed details of village life and superstitions'.

We have also discussed films by directors Girish Kasaravelli and G. V. Iyer. Kasaravalli concerned himself with the 'stifling Brahminical orthodoxy that cloaks itself in puritanical ritual' and explores this theme in *Ghata Shradhdha* (The Ritual, 1977). Iyer's *Adi Shankaracharya* (1983), which won him the Golden Lotus, was the first feature film to be made in Sanskrit and is a tribute to the eighth century sage Shankara who, in the words of Garga (1996: 284), 'expounded the Advaita (non dualist) philosophy and who is to Hinduism what Saint Thomas Aquinas is to Christianity'.

Of the handful of women film directors in India who have gained national recognition, Prema Karanth is from Karnataka. We have discussed how her touching account of a child-widow, *Phaniyamma* (1982), so poignantly illustrates the problem of young widowhood (Garga 1996: 285). However, despite the outstanding success of such film directors, Kannada artistic cinema has yet to achieve international repute or to produce filmmakers of the calibre of those working in Malayalam cinema. Nor is it likely to do so while it continues to play safe.

For decades, Kannada cinema drew on the wealth of literature in the language. But recently its filmmakers have taken the soft option and settled for remakes of Tamil, Telugu and Malayalam hits. Many of the commercially successful Kannada releases in 2002/3, notably *Kotikobba* (One in a Million) and *Raktha Kaneeru* (Tears of Blood), are adaptations of Tamil films. The efforts of the Karnataka's government to discourage this trend by imposing a steep entertainment tax on remakes have failed to discourage the practice.

Consequently, contemporary Kannada cinema has lost much of the sheen of the successes of the 1970s, notably *Vamsa Vriksha* (Family Tree), jointly directed by B.V. Karanth and Girish Karnad, G.V. Iyer's *Hansa Geethe* (Swan Song) and those mentioned earlier: Pattabhi Rama Reddy's *Samskara*, Girish Karnad's *Kaadu*, and B.V. Karanth's *Chomana Dudi*.

Girish Kasaravalli, who has steadfastly worked outside its commercial film scene, is currently Kannada cinema's only internationally recognised name. He has produced a formidable body of work which includes *Ghata Shradhdha* (see page 131) and also *Tabarana Kathe* (Tabara's Tale, 1986) and *Dweepa* (Island, 2001).

Tamil Cinema

Tamil cinema, too, is not known for serious and artistic films. It is characterised by its mawkish sentimentality and its strong link with politics. This connection between politics and cinema is perhaps the most noteworthy feature of the cinema of Tamil Nadu, since political figures such as M.G. Ramachandran and Jayalalitha used their work in cinema to establish their public identities.

During the past nine decades of development, Tamil cinema has appealed to movie-goers in Tamil Nadu and in neighbouring countries like Sri Lanka, Singapore and Malaysia where substantial numbers of Tamil-speaking people live. *Chandralekha* (1948) established the Tamil popular tradition of filmmaking and became a sensational success throughout India and beyond. Directed by S.S.Vasan, *Chandralekha* is a spectacular dance drama revolving around two royal brothers who fight for the throne and the hand of a beautiful maiden. It represents the clash of good and evil.

Tamil cinema plays a role in the public sphere and has forged strong links with local politics. One cannot understand the hugely significant role of the DMK (*Dravida Munnetra Kazhagam*) in south Indian politics without reference to Tamil cinema. A film like *Parasakthi* (The Goddess, 1952), with its unconcealed antipathy to the Congress Party and the authority exercised by the brahmin caste, illustrates this phenomenon. Films such as *Parasakthi, Velakkari* (Maid, 1949) and *Oor Iravu* (One Night, 1951) made direct interventions into politics. Scriptwriters C.N. Annadurai and M. Karunanidhi succeeded in injecting their politics into cinema. In many of these films, party symbols are on display and playful use is made in the dialogue of the names of party leaders. In certain films such as *Panam* (Money, 1952) and *Thangaratnam* (1978) the narrative was interwoven with documentary footage of party meetings. Tamil cinema and local politics were inseparably linked. This is clear from the rise to political power and cinematic superstardom of M.G. Ramachandran (MGR), who was the chief minister of Tamil Nadu from 1977-1987 and was mythologised by his fans as the patron saint of the poor. Another important aspect of Tamil cinema is that there is no clear-cut distinction between art cinema and popular cinema as there is in Malayalam cinema. The most talented Tamil filmmakers, like Mani Rathnam, seek to realise their creations within the parameters of popular cinema.

Around the 1980s, the cinematic quality of Tamil films improved remarkably. This was facilitated by the establishment of the Madras film institute. Hariharan and Balu Mahendra and other graduates of this institute spearheaded this new trend. Much credit is due to director Mani Rathnam whose films, among them *Roja* (1992), *Bombay* (1994) and *Kannathil Muthamittal* (A Peck on the Cheek, 2002) have generated international attention. Rathnam has graduated from regional cinema to international cinema. His main preoccupation – the human face of terrorism be it in Kashmir or Bombay or Sri Lanka – has aroused much interest among movie-goers in India and beyond. His sophisticated representational strategies and cinematic techniques that combine Hollywood, MTV, commercial art and Bollywood deserve closer study.

As well as directors, certain actors in Tamil cinema such as Kamal Hassan and Rajnikant have begun to acquire national recognition. The film *Muthu* (Pearl, 2000) has catapulted Rajnikant into international stardom and was very popular in Japan.

Malayalam Cinema

The cinema of Kerala has achieved international recognition, due to distinguished Malayalam film directors such as Adoor Gopalakrishnan, G.

Aravindan and Shaji Karun. While popular films that bear the imprint of melodramatic musicals are produced in large numbers, the artistic cinema continues to grow. Kerala's literacy rates are the highest in India and there is a strong literary and theatre tradition that has aided this film culture.

Gopalakrishnan's *Elippathayam* (Rat Trap, 1981), brought him international recognition and the British Film Institute Award as the 'maker of the most original and imaginative film' (Garga 1996: 271). His films such as *Chemmeen* (The Shrimp, 1968), *Mukhamukham* (Face to Face, 1984), *Ananthram* (Monologue, 1987) explore the concept of the self and the struggle to adapt to changing social circumstances.

The talent of the late G. Aravindan is evident in *Thampu* (The Circus Tent, 1978), *Kummaty* (The Bogeyman, 1979), *Esthappan* (Stephen, 1980) and *Pokkuveyil* (Twilight, 1981). *Thampu* explores the complex and lonely lives of circus-players 'with an almost documentary fidelity'. *Kummaty* deals with the legendary figure of a mysterious wizard who figures in children's lore in Kerala. Aravindan presents this character and children's reactions to him with poetic charm. *Esthappan* is set among Christian fishermen in Kerala and narrates the life of a wandering and mysterious spiritualist. *Pokkuveyil* is about a young poet who, unable to withstand the hard realities of life, slips into a world of fantasy and hallucination. The film has very little dialogue and relies on a rich use of colour. We have already discussed his *Chidambaram* (1985). This and his last film *Vasthuhara* (Dispossessed, 1990) confirm his sensitivity as a film maker.

Shaji Karun, already distinguished as a cameraman, emerged as a talented film director with his first feature film, *Piravi* (The Birth, 1988). Based on the Rajan murder case during the Emergency in the mid-1970s, it explores with great poetic sensitivity and cinematic understanding the anguished search of an old man for his lost son, who is reported to have been taken into police custody. *Piravi* won several prestigious awards at international film festivals and was shown in England on Channel 4.

While these filmmakers were making artistic films, the popular cinema in Kerala was catering to the escapist taste of the bulk of film goers, producing cheap entertainment. These films offer romance, sex, seduction and murder in abundance. As in many other states, the film industry in Kerala has had its ups and downs. At one point, money poured in from the Gulf states to shore up its film production but this is no longer the case. As with most popular cinema, the appeal of the films depends largely on the drawing power of the actors and actresses. In Kerala, actors such as Mammooty and Mohanlall, who have acted in hundreds of films, are eagerly sought by film producers.

But Malayalam cinema deserves attention for its enriching of the artistic tradition of film. And recent releases confirm this.

Probably the most demanding of the eighteen films that made up the 2003 Indian Panorama was Adoor Gopalakrishnan's *Nizhalkkuthu* (Shadow Kill). It is a film that explores the recesses of human consciousness in a way that few filmmakers can achieve. Gopalakrishnan explores the life of a hangman, Kaliyappan, a human being wrecked by memories of the many people he has hanged and especially one innocent young man hanged 25 years ago. What makes this film a gem is that it is a moving moral allegory. It addresses the questions of human responsibility and freedom through the tale of this guilt-ridden hangman of princely Travancore province in the pre-Independence era.

The characterisation is rich in contrasts: the hangman's rope which kills the condemned also cures the sick. The rope has curative powers: when burnt before an image of Goddess Kali it yields a magical ash that can drive away human ailments. The hangman himself is a reflection of the Goddess Kali: he is both destroyer and protector. As he cures others, he himself sinks further and further into mental anguish and physical indisposition. The dichotomy inherent in his condition is underscored throughout the film (see Chatterjee in *Hindustan Times* 17/09/2003 for a comprehensive account).

Telugu Cinema

Telugu cinema, too, has little to offer by way of serious and artistic work, although Hyderabad (Telugu) is one of the three most important film centres in India in terms of the number of films produced. The vast majority of Telugu films – mythological films as well as social dramas – are trite, highly melodramatic, often stagey, and are not known for the exploration of complex human experiences.

For many years N.T. Rama Rao, former Chief Minister of Andhra Pradesh, dominated the Telugu screen. He acted in over three hundred films and was well known for his portrayal of religious figures. In recent years, one or two determined filmmakers such as Narasinga Rao, have sought to introduce a serious note to Telugu cinema. In his first film *Rangula Kala* (A Colourful Dream, 1983), he plays the lead. The film portrays the tormented sensibility of a highly gifted modern painter, Ravi, and his growing social awareness and political consciousness. His film, *Dasi* (Bonded Woman, 1988) won five national awards and gained him national recognition as a distinguished film-maker in India. *Dasi* deals with the way in which young girls from poor peasant families were bought by rich families as bonded labour. But despite the best efforts of artists like Narasinga Rao, Telugu cinema, with its large annual film output, has yet to develop a sophisticated film culture.

Marathi Cinema

Many film historians would designate Maharashtra as the birthplace of Indian cinema. The name of D.G. Phalke is honoured as the father of Indian cinema. Early on, there were a number of Marathi film directors who showed talent and commitment to the growth of Indian film culture. V. Shantaram, Damle, Fatehlal, Master Vinayak and also P.L. Deshpande, G.D. Madgulkar, Raja Paranjpe and Sudhir Phadke are perhaps most significant. However, as an art form and industry it has had its share of problems: Most films made in Marathi are cheap and commercial, often modelled on Hindi films, and they cater to the escapist desires of the majority of film-goers. In terms of experience, style and technique, there is little to recommend them. However, despite this commercial film culture, a number of directors have recently sought to create a vibrant artistic cinema in Maharashtra, among them Jabhar Patel, Amol Palekar, Nachiket and Jayoo Patwardhan and Vijaya Metha.

Jabbar Patel, a physician by profession, has been closely involved with the theatre. His first film. *Samna* (The Confrontation, 1975), based on a script by Vijay Tendulkar, dramatises the conflict of wills between a small-town political racketeer and a morally upright school teacher. His next film, *Jait Re Jait* (The Victory, 1977) tells the story of a tribal youth, 'the son of a village oracle, who loses faith in his god when his father dies of a snake bite and his fiancée is stung to death by the poisonous bees from the holy mountain' (Garga, 1996: 293). But the film that perhaps established most strongly Jabbar Patel's reputation for serious moral concern was *Umbartha* (The Threshold, 1981). The film centres on the life of Sulabha, a young woman who has a diploma in social work and is married into an upper middle class family. Her mother-in-law, herself a social worker, would like Sulabha to join her in her work. But Sulabha accepts a position at an office some three hundred miles from her home. She has a husband and a five year old daughter, but she is equally attracted to her job and the film charts the way that she negotiates these conflicting loyalties.

Nachitet and Jayoo Patwardhan's *22 June 1897* (1979) cinematises a violent episode in Indian history. Damodar Chapekar, the eldest of three sons of a preacher singer, leads a group of militant Brahmin youths who are determined to challenge two of the elements of British imperialism – the English language and Christianity. Damodar plans to kill Walter Rand, a British officer and the film deals with this incident and its aftermath.

Like Prema Karanth in Karnataka, Vijaya Metha is a distinguished woman film director. Her film *Smriti Chitre* (Episodes from Memory, 1983) won the National Award for the best Marathi language film of that year and constitutes a probing examination of the Brahmin tradition as a cultural force.

Amol Palekar acted in Basu Chatterji's *Rajnigandha* (1994) and his first film *Akriet* (The Misbegotten, 1981) won many awards at international film festivals. The film is based on a series of violent murders among tribals in Maharashtra. In 1990, he produced *Thodasa Rumani Ho Jaye* (Let's Get Romantic), a mass-entertainment musical. So there is a handful of Marathi filmmakers who are seeking to improve the quality of Marathi filmmaking, many of whom have also directed Hindi films. However, a fall from favour was reflected in the dwindling number of films produced in the 1990s. Thirty five Marathi films were produced in 1993, 25 in 1994, 21 in 1995 and only 10 in 1996.

But the new millennium has been good for Marathi cinema in terms of both quality and commercial breakthroughs and there are recent signs of a resurgence. The directing/writing duo of Sumitra Bhave and Sunil Sukthankar has played a key role in both. The first film they made was the superbly crafted *Vaskrupurush* (Guardian Spirit of the House), about a successful doctor who returns to his village home after forty years, to reconnect with the guardian spirit of the house. Then followed the hugely popular *Dahavi F* (Standard Tenth F), a well-acted, sharply written narrative of a group of schoolboys who struggle to surmount their disadvantageous background.

The release late in 2003 of Amol Palekar's *Anaahat* (Eternity) in a New Delhi multiplex represents a huge step forward for contemporary Marathi cinema. Never before has a film made in this language been accorded such attention outside Maharashtra.

Anaahat is set in the 10th century BC in a kingdom whose ruler is incapable of fathering a heir to the throne. So, in keeping with the old practice called *Niyoga*, the queen is ordered by the Senate to seek a sexual partner for a night so that she can bear a child. She goes out much against her wishes, only to discover the unplumbed depths of her own sexuality. Her relationship with her husband changes completely.

The successes of these recent films suggest that Marathi cinema is beginning to make its presence felt once again at national level.

Bengali Cinema

Of all the regional cinemas it is Bengal that won for Indian cinema widespread international acclaim. We have already considered three of the most important and famous Bengali film directors: Satyajit Ray, Ritwik Ghatak and Mrinal Sen. Of the young and promising filmmakers, we have also discussed Goutam Ghosh's *Antarjali Yatra* (The Voyage Beyond, 1987) and Aparna Sen's *36 Chowringhee Lane* (1981).

Most critics, when writing about regional cinemas in India, will focus on Bengali cinema. A rich film culture continues to characterise Bengali cinema and the very active film society movement played a significant role in shaping the peoples's taste and widening their cinematic horizons. The interaction between the literary culture and film culture was also beneficial. Mahatma Gandhi is reported to have said that what Bengal thinks today, the rest of India thinks tomorrow. In much the same way, Bengali cinema has led in subject matter from the 1920s till the middle of the 1940s. And the way Rabindranath Tagore's work has been creatively used by Satyajit Ray and others enhances the film culture. Garga (1996: 307) rightly asserts that:

In a situation where much of Indian cinema is homogenised and moribund, the regional film has given it an identity and a sense of purpose. It has also revealed the variety of peoples and cultures in India with their richly diverse languages, legends, stories, clothes, climate, music and dance.

The tradition of excellence continues. At the 2003 National Awards in Delhi, at least two Bengali films – Abhijit Chaudhuri's *Patalghar* (The Underground Chamber) and Subhadro Chowdhury's *Prohor* (The Course of Time) show what an infusion of new blood can do to revitalise a cinema that has been groping in the dark for some time.

World class in terms of technique and production values, these two films – one an ambitious 'sci-fi' thriller, the other a minimalist probe into the mind of a young woman who is grappling with the trauma of rape – have unveiled the depth of the talent pool that seems to be flourishing in Kolkata (Calcutta).

Patalghar is about a scientist who stumbles upon the existence of a lost device, and a little boy who inherits a sprawling mansion in the countryside. The device is a gun that can put a person to sleep for decades and which is hidden in a secret underground chamber of the mansion. The harmonious mix of the physical attributes of the real world and the confounding details of the realms of fantasy has resulted in a constantly riveting film.

Much smaller in scope is *Prohor*. It tells the story of a nurse haunted by a traumatic act of violence that tore apart her happy little world six years before. Certain factors make this an interesting film:

• The story eschews physical trauma, opting to present the unfolding of events through the inner psychological dynamics of the central character and an evocative soundtrack

• The beauty of the camerawork – the colour palette, the texture, the quality of the lighting and the depth of focus – suggests craftsmanship of the highest order.

Technical progress has for years been the stock in trade of Bengali directors like Buddhadeb Dasgupta, Goutam Ghose and Rituparno Ghosh. Indeed, Rituparno Ghosh's recent *Chokher Bali* (Sand in the Eye, 2003) is playing to packed houses in Kolkata. It stars Aishwarya Rai in the role of Binodini, a Bengali widow who dares to place her sexual needs above societal constraints. Ghosh's success as a skilled storyteller is in the Satyajit Ray mould. These recent films announce the advent of a new breed of cinema professionals who have the power to bring about dramatic change in the Kolkata filmmaking scene.

Missing from our discussion of India's regional cinemas is Punjabi cinema, which has suffered substantially since partition and deserves support and encouragement.

CHAPTER 9

Conclusion

This chapter offers critical reflection on the developments described and analysed in this updated account of Indian popular cinema. Hindi cinema has increasingly come to be called Bollywood, thanks mainly to Western media. But the epithet does not do the industry justice. As Joshi (2002) noted:

> Calling it 'Bollywood' fails to reflect its diversity and range... Although many film artists and critics of Indian origin consider it a product of negative stereotyping, it is part of the language used by Indian cable television networks all over the globe, with their heavy emphasis on Hindi cinema-based programmes and chat shows. (p.75)

The phenomenon of Bollywood now commands attention worldwide and requires examining. Bollywood is a neologism, a conflation of the words Hollywood and Bombay cinema. It refers mainly to the commercial cinema associated with Bombay. It is widely believed that Indian cinema and Bollywood are co-terminous. Although there is much overlap, we can make an analytically useful distinction between the two. In analytical terms, Bollywood is both less and more than Indian cinema. Less because it is confined to Bombay commercial films, whereas Indian cinema, which has evolved over almost a century, consists of the art tradition as expressed in the works of such directors as Satyajit Ray and Adoor Gopalakrishnan, the various regional cinemas such as Bengal, Kerala and Assam and also the larger traditions of popular cinema in Tamil Nadu and Andra Pradesh.

But Bollywood is also more than Indian cinema because it covers a larger area of cinematic reach – distribution and consumption – promoted by VCRs, DVDs, websites and satellite television. To put it rather simplistically, Indian cinema is largely driven by internal imperatives while Bollywood draws its energy from external sources and resources. What is important here is the interconnection between Indians and Bollywood cinemas. We are currently seeing the 'Bollywoodisation' of Indian cinema, and this has much to do with globalisation.

The diasporic Indians slot into the interconnection between Indians and Bollywood cinema. How does one conceptualise the contributions of diasporic Indian filmmakers discussed here in Chapter 7? A recent study by Naficy (2003) offers an exciting overview of filmmaking in the postcolonial, developing world. Its blurb and the endorsement by David Morley observe that

> How their personal experiences of exile or diaspora translate into cinema is a key focus of Naficy's work. Although the experience of expatriation varies greatly from one person to the next, the films themselves exhibit stylistic similarities, from their open and closed form aesthetics to their nostalgia and memory-driven multilingual narratives, and from their emphasis on political agency to their concern with identity and transgression of identity...

Comparing them to Hollywood films, Naficy calls these diasporic films 'accented'. Their account results from the displacement of the filmmakers, their alternative production modes, and their style. Accented cinema is an emerging genre, one that demands new viewing skills from audiences.

Discerning lovers of popular Hindi films have never had it so good. In the star system-driven Mumbai film industry, individual personalities do matter, but the last decade will be remembered particularly for the changes to the profile shown by the Hindi film audience, and for the impact these crucial developments had on the textual content and textual features of popular films. During the decade, the broad thematic concerns and the technical attributes – if not the overall narrative grammar – of Hindi mainstream cinema metamorphosed significantly.

By the mid-1990s, aided no doubt by the process of economic liberalisation, a new phalanx of directors who were equally ready to embrace global influences established their credentials as exceptional craftsmen. Mansoor Khan (veteran producer Nasir Hussein's son), Aditya Chopra (Yash Chopra's elder son), Sooraj Barjatya of the Rajshri family, and Karen Johar (producer Yash Johar's son) spearheaded the charge of the youth brigade. They shunned the blind, all-out Hollywood fixation of their predecessors. Instead, they invented a median mode of filmmaking and storytelling, and crafted some of the decade's biggest hits: *Jo Jecta Wohi Sikandar* (Winner Takes All); *Dilwale Dulhania Le Jayenge*; *Hum Aapke Hain Koun!* and *Kuch Kuch Hota Hai*.

There were more women directors both in India and in the Indian diaspora. The diasporic women filmmakers are going from strength to strength. In the words of Griffin (2003): Mira Nair and Gurinder Chadha try to combine their engagement 'with the elsewhere and the other rather than with the here and now and the diasporic realities' in contemporary USA and Britain (see Griffin, 2003: 377, for a useful discussion of the cultural imaginary among contemporary Black and Asian women playwrights in Britain). In an interview with Antonio Monda (Spinelli, 2002: 115-117), Mira Nair states that the effects of globalisation can be seen not only in Bollywood films but also in *Monsoon Wedding*.

> One of the reasons I wanted to do *Monsoon Wedding* was because I wanted to talk about people who live their non evolving culture with pride, and without a sense of inferiority. When I was a teenager, like all my contemporaries, I loved the Beatles' songs, ignoring completely Indian music. I felt the same way about my country's cinema, which as you know has some extraordinary masters. (p115)

The films emanating from Indian directors and producers are marked by a newly perfected blend of Hollywood-style gloss and an indigenous narrative ethos. These films are aimed at an audience that increasingly looks towards the West for its material needs, but instinctively turns inwards for self-assurance at the first perceived threat to its cultural identity.

Concerns have been expressed about some of the negative aspects of globalisation on the Indian film audience. These relate to media imperialism/cultural imperialism. The media imperialism approach suggests a one-way flow of cultural production from the developed to the developing world as significantly affecting the role of the media in many countries (Tunstall, 1977; Katz and Wedell, 1978; Lee, 1981). Neo-marxists prefer the term cultural imperialism since they find the term media imperialism too constricting (Schiller, 1976; Mattelart, 1979). This argument has been criticised by writers such as Tomlinson (1991) and Schlesinger (1991), who argue that countries (like India) do not necessarily act as cultural sponges – hence the emphasis on the interplay between the local and the global mentioned in our introduction to this book.

Relevant to this debate is the changing nature of Mumbai cinema's texts and subtexts – the multiplex allows the English-speaking minority audience to be catered for. The 1990s saw the screening in Mumbai of *Jurassic Park*; *Speed; True Lies; Titanic* and *Godzilla,* among others. These films partly achieved their principal goal: widening the audience base for American films in India. The huge success of *Jurassic Park* and *Titanic* gave Bollywood a scare but, as always, the indigenous 'potboiler' continues to have a clear edge in the Indian market.

It is evident from our discussion and analysis of recent developments in Indian popular cinema that the last twelve years have thrown up huge contradictions. Music, romance and a degree of realism made a triumphal return to mainstream cinema after an entire decade when action-oriented, on-screen violence in films became more insistent and more graphic than ever before. Though traditional family values and cultural orthodoxy became the dominant mantra, Hindi films with their stress on foreign locales succumbed to the lures of westernisation. Into this frame have entered diasporic Indian filmmakers and musicians with different texts and subtexts. Attempts to uphold traditional culture, such as not showing kissing on screen, have met with fierce resistance from directors – this prompted *Life* magazine into devoting a rare cover to India entitled 'India's kissing crisis'. The editorial view of *India Today* (2002) that 'it is hypocrisy raised to the level of an art form' is entirely fitting. The role of the satellite channels which telecast soap operas such as *Tara*, with its portrayal of sexual openness and promiscuity, is becoming increasingly significant.

With A.R. Rahman of *Bombay Dreams* having been chosen to write the score for the most expensive theatre production ever – the £8 million musical of *Lord of the Rings* due to open in 2005 (Leitch, 2003: 22) and the picture of Aishwarya Rai adorning the cover of *Time* magazine (the Asia edition of 27 October, 2003), Indian popular cinema is on the world stage.

The broad survey of the terrain sketched in this book is intended primarily for the general reader with little knowledge of Indian cinema, as well as for the better informed. Our audience is primarily British and American, although we hope students and readers from elsewhere will also find it useful. We have not sought to discuss or even list all of the significant films made in India during the past ten decades, but have chosen to focus rather on some representative examples that delineate the broad contours of Indian cinema.

Although our focus of interest has been on popular cinema, this is best understood in relation to artistic cinema. So along with popular cinema we have discussed artistic cinema in India, as a way of pointing out the significant differences and occasional affinities of interest.

Throughout the book, we have sought to situate Indian films in their cultural context. Films open up a window onto the wider world. By watching Indian films and exploring them sensitively, we can attain a deeper understanding of Indian culture and of its history, politics and values. This approach has allowed us to point out the distinctiveness of Indian cinema more clearly and contextualise contemporary films more productively.

In the final analysis, what is most important is that we begin to see and appreciate Indian films with enhanced critical understanding. This book has been written in that hope. By watching Indian films, not only will we understand Indian society and culture better but also, through comparisons and contrasts, the society and culture in which we live.

Appendix

NFDC Bombay
Number of films sold and revenue from key export markets for Indian films, 1988

Country	No. of films	Revenue (Rs)
Arabian Gulf	179	24,349,000
USSR	18	9,811,000
Indonesia	41	9,484,000
Sri Lanka	30	2,588,000
Burma	17	2,463,00
UK & Ireland	67	2,286,000
Morocco	36	2,031,000
Jordan	28	1,814,000
Fiji Islands	29	1,785,000
Singapore	27	1,642,000
Mauritius	61	1,632,000
Sudan	31	1,288,000
Tanzania	28	1,281,000
Maldives	27	1,214,000
Kenya	22	1,086,000
Malaysia	33	808,000
Yemen, Djibouti, Sanna	13	761,000
West Indies	13	590,000
South/Latin America	12	524,000
Gambia	11	536,000
Nigeria	10	451,000
Liberia	10	331,000

Source: *NFDC, Bombay. From the Asian Film Industry* by John A. Lent (1990) London: C. Helm.

Recommended Reading

The following books are recommended for further reading.

Chakravarty, Sumita S. (1993) *National Identity in Indian Popular Cinema 1947-1987* Austin: University of Texas Press

Dwyer, R. (2000) *All You Want Is Money, All You Need Is Love* London: Cassell

Dwyer, R. and Patel, D. (2002) *Culture of Hindi Film* New Delhi: Oxford University Press

Joshi, L.M. (ed.) (2002) *Bollywood: Popular Indian Cinema* London: Dakini Books

Kabir, Munni (2002) *Bollywood: The Indian Cinema Story* Basingstoke: Macmillan

Mishra, V. (2002) *Bollywood Cinema Temples of Desire* London: Routledge

Nandy, A. (ed.)(1998) *The Secret Politics of Our Desires. Innocence, Culpability and Indian Popular Cinema* London: Zed Books

Prasad, M.M. (1998) *Ideology of the Hindi Film: a Historical Reconstruction* Delhi: Oxford University Press

Vasudevan, R. (2000) *Making Meaning in Indian Cinema* New Delhi: Oxford University Press

Virdi, J. (2003) *The Cinematic ImagiNation* New Jersey: Rutgers University Press

References

Armes, R. (1987) *Third World Film Making and the West* Berkeley: University of California Press

Arnold, A. (1988) 'Popular Film Song In India: A Case of Mass Market Musical Eclecticism' in *Popular Music* Vol.7 No.2 May pp.177-188

Arnold, A. (1991) 'Hindi Film Git' Doctoral Dissertation submitted to the University of Illinois at Urbana-Champaign

Arnold, D. and Hardiman, D. (Eds) (1994) 'Subaltern Studies' Vol. VIII Delhi: Oxford University Press

Arora, P. (1995) 'Imperilling the Prestige of the White Woman Colonial Anxiety' in *Visual Anthropology Review and Film Censorship in British India* Vol.II No.2 Fall pp. 36-50

Ashcroft, Bill, Griffiths, G. and Tiffin, H. (eds.) (1995) *The Post-Colonial Studies Reader* London: Routledge

Baily, J. (1995) 'The Role of Music in Three British Muslim Communities' in *Diaspora* Vol.1 No.4 pp. 77-88

Banerji, S. (1988) 'Ghazals to Bhangra in Great Britain' in *Popular Music* Vol.7 No.2 pp. 207-214

Barnouw, E. and Krishnaswamy, S. (1963) *Indian Film* New York: Columbia University Press

Basu, S, Kak, S. and Krishen, P. (1980) 'Cinema and Society: A Search for Meaning in a New Genre' in Krishen, P. (Ed) *India International Centre Quarterly* Vol.8, No.1, March pp. 57-76

Beeman, W.O. (1980) 'The use of Music in Popular Film: East and West' in Krishen, P. (Ed) *India International Centre Quarterly* Vol.8, No.1, March pp. 77-88

Bharucha, R. (1995) *Chandralekha Woman Dance Resistance* New Delhi: Harper Collins

Bhattacharya, R. (1990) 'Breaking Mind Blocks about Documentaries' in *Montreal Serai* April/May

Bhattacharya, G. and Gabriel, J. (1994) 'Gurinder Chadha and the Apna Generation' in *Third Text* Nol.27 Summer pp. 55-63

Bhowmick, S. (1995) 'Film Censorship' in Maitra P. (Ed) *100 years of Cinema*, Calcutta: Nandan

Binford, M.R. (1989) 'Indian Popular Cinema' in *Quarterly Review of Film and Video* Vol.II, pp.1-9

Brah, A. (1996) *Cartographies of Diaspora: Contesting Identities* London: Routledge

Braziel, J.E. and Mannur, A. (eds.) (2003) *Theorizing Diaspora: A Reader* Oxford: Blackwell

Brown, J. (1994) *Modern India* Second Edition, Oxford: Oxford University Press

Bruce, S. (1995) *Religion in Modern Britain* Oxford University Press

Chakraborty, C. (2003) Subaltern Studies, Bollywood and Lagaan *Economic and Political Weekly* 10 May p1879-1884

Chakravarty, S.S. (1989) 'National Identity and the Realist Aesthetic: Indian Cinema of the Fifties' in *Quarterly Review of Film and Video* Vol.11, pp.31-48

Chakravarty, S.S. (1996) *National Identity in Indian Popular Cinema* (1947-1987) Delhi: Oxford University Press

Chandra, M. (1973) *The World of Courtesans* Delhi: Oxford University Press

Chandra, M. (1994) 'Music Mania' in *India Today* November 15.

Chatterjee, G. (1992) *Awara* New Delhi: Wiley Eastern Ltd

Chatterjee, P. (1993) *The Nation and its Fragments* Princeton: Princeton University Press

Chatterjee, P. (1994) 'The Indian Documentary Scene Fraught with Hazards' in *Cinemaya* No.23 pp. 44-45

Chatterjee, P. (1995) 'A Bit of Song and Dance' in VASUDEV, A. (Ed) *Frames of Mind* New Delhi: UBPSD

Chatterjee, S. (2003) Nizhalkkuthu: Vintage Adoor *The Hindustan Times* 17 September

Chatterji, S. A. (1997) 'The Politics of Parallel Cinema' in *Deep Focus* Vol.VII No.1 pp. 74-82

Danda, D. (1997) 'Bandit Queen – A Semiotic Approach' in *Deep Focus* Vol.II No.2 pp 34-40

Das Gupta, C. (1991) *The Painted Face: Studies in India's Popular Cinema* New Delhi: Roli Books

Das, V. (1988) 'Shakti Versus Sati – A Reading of the Santoshi Ma Cult' in *Manushi* No.49, pp. 26-30

Derné, S. and Jadwin, L. (2000) Male Hindi Filmgoers' Gaze: an ethnographic interpretation *Contributions to Indian Sociology* Volume 34 Number 2

Dharap, B. V. (1973) *Indian Films Pune*: Motion Picture Enterprise

Dhillon-Kashyap, D. (1988) 'Locating the Asian Experience' in *Screen* Vol.29, No.4, Autumn pp. 120-126

Dhondy, F. (1985) 'Keeping Faith: Indian Film and its World' in *Daedalus* Fall, pp. 125-140

Dissayanake, W. (Ed) (1988) *Cinema and Cultural Identity: Reflection on Films from Japan, Indian and China* Lanham: University Press of America

Dissayanake, W. and Sahai, M. (1992) *Sholay: A Cultural Reading* Honolulu: Wiley: East West

Dissayanake, W. (1993) (Ed) *Melodrama and Asian Cinema* Cambridge: Cambridge University Press

Doraiswamy, R. (1994) 'Changing Narrative Strategies' in *Cinemaya* No.23 pp. 4-12

Dubey, S. (1992) The Middle Class, in Gordon, L.A. and Oldenburg, P. (eds.) *India Briefing* Boulder, Co.: Westview Press p137-164

Dudrah, Rajinder K. (2002) Drum 'n' dhol *European Journal of Cultural Studies* Volume 5 Number 3 p363-383

Dutt, S. (1997) 'A Great Indian, a Great Man' in *Screen* 20 June

Dwyer, R. (2000) *All You Want is Money, All You Need is Love* London: Cassell

Filmmaker (2002) Interview with Mira Nair Volume 10 Number 2 Winter p78

Garga, B. D, (1996) *So Many Cinemas* Mumba: Eminence Designs

Geetha, J. (1990) 'The Mutating Mother' in *Deep Focus* Vol.III,1 No.3 pp.9-15

Ghosh, B. (1992) 'Satyajit Raj's Devi: Constructing a Third World Feminist – Critique' in *Screen* Vol.33 No.2 Summer pp.165-173

Gilroy. P. (1991) *There Ain't No Black in the Union Jack: The Cultural Politics of Race and Nationalism* London: Hutchinson

Gilroy, P. (1993) *The Black Atlantic* Cambridge: Harvard University Press

Gokulsing, K.Moti (2004) *Soft-Soaping India: The World of Indian Televised Soap Operas* Staffordshire UK and Sterling USA: Trentham Books

Gopalan, L. (1997) Avenging Women in Indian Cinema' in *Screen* Vol.38, No.1, pp. 42-59

Gopinath, G. (1995) 'Bombay, U.K. Yuba City' Bhangra Music and the Engendering of Diaspora in *Diaspora* Vol.4 No.3 pp. 303-321

Gopinath, G. (2003) Nostalgia, Desire, Diaspora: South Asian Sexualities in Motion in Braziel, J.E. and Mannur, A. (eds.) *Theorizing Diaspora: A Reader* Oxford: Blackwell

Griffin, G. (2003) Constitutive Subjectivities: Contemporary Black and Asian Women Playwrights in Britain *The European Journal of Women's Studies* Volume 10 Number 4 p377-394

Gulzar, Nihalani, D. and Chatterjee, S. (2003) *Encyclopaedia of Hindi Cinema* New Delhi: Encyclopaedia Britannica

Gupta, B. S. (1997) 'India in the Twenty-First Century' in *International Affairs* Vol.73 No.2 pp. 297-314

Hardgrave, Jr R. L. (1975) *When Stars Displace the Gods: The Folk Culture of Cinema in Tamil Nadu* in Occasional Paper Series No.2 Centre for Asian Studies – University of Texas, pp. 1-23

Hayward, S. (Second edition) (2000) *Cinema Studies: the Key Concepts* London: Routledge

Housden, R. (1996) *Travels Through Sacred India* New Delhi: Harper Collins

IMAX, (1996) *A Bigger Vision – Celebrating 100 Years of Cinema* London: British Film Institute

India Today (2002) Is Sex ok? 5 August

Jain, R. D. (1960) *The Economic Aspects of the Film Industry in India* Delhi: Atma Ram and Sons

Jha, S.K. (2001) The New Patriot *The Hindustan Times* 5 October

Joseph, A. and Sharma, K. (Ed) (1994) *Whose News? The Media and Women's Issues* New Delhi: Sage

Joshi, L.M. (2002) The Power of Popular Hindi Cinema, in Spinelli, I. (ed.) *Indian Summer* Milano: Edizioni Olivares

Kabir, M. N. (1991) *Indian Film Music* Postgraduate Seminar Aspects of Commonwealth Literature – Institute of Commonwealth Studies, University of London, 21 October

Kabir, M. N. and Snell, R. (1994) 'Bollywood Nights: The Voices Behind the Stars of Indian Film Music' in Broughton, S., Ellingham, M., Muddyman, D. and Trillo, R. (Eds) *World Music – The Rough Guide* London: Rough Guides Ltd.

Kakar, S. (1996) *The Indian Psyque* Delhi: Oxford University Press

Kapoor, R. (1997) 'Quote ... Unquote' in *Filmfare* June

Katz, E. and Weddell, G. (1978) *Broadcasting in the Third World* Cambridge: Harvard University Press

Kaviraj, S. (1994) 'Crisis of the Nation-State in India' in *Political Studies XLII*, pp. 115-129

Kazmi, N. (1996) *Ire in the Soul – Bollywood's Angry Years* New Delhi: Harper Collins

Khanna, S. (1980) 'Indian Cinema and Indian Life Vol.III of Hindi-Urdu Films for instructional purposes. Centers for South and Southeast Asia Studies, Berkeley: University of California

Kohli, A. (1990) *Democracy and Discontent: India's Growing Crisis of Governability* Cambridge: Cambridge University Press

Kothari, R. (1988) *State Against Democracy* New Delhi: Ajanta Publication

Krishen, P. (1980) 'Indian Popular Cinema Myth, Meaning and Metaphor' *Indian International Centre* Quarterly Special Issue, Vol.8, No.1, March

Lee, C. (1981) *Media Imperialism Reconsidered: The Homogeneity of Television* Beverley Hills, CA: Sage

Leitch, L. (2003) From Bombay Dreams to Middle-Earth Fantasy *Evening Standard* 21 October p22

Levich, J. (1997) 'The undiscovered Art of Ritwik Ghatak' in *Film Comment* Vol.33 No.2 March/April pp. 30-35

Long, R.E. (New Revised Edition, 1997) *The Films of Merchant Ivory* New York: Harry N. Abrams

Macey, D (2000) *The Penguin Dictionary of Critical Theory* London: Penguin Books

Macnab, G. (2002) Interview with director Mira Nair *Sight and Sound* January Volume 12 Number 1 p18-20

Madan, T. N. (1989) 'Religion in India' in *Proceedings of the American Academy of Arts and Sciences* Vol.118, No.4, pp. 115-146

Maitra, P. (Ed) (1995) *100 Years of Cinema* Calcutta: Nandan.

Majumdar, D. (1995) Indian Film Industry in MAITRA, P. (Ed) *100 years of Cinema* Calcutta: Nandan

Majumdar, B. (2001) Politics of Leisure in Colonial India, 'Lagaan': Invocation of a Lost History? *Economic and Political Weekly* 1 September p3399-3404

Mankekar, P. (1999) *Screening Culture, Viewing Politics* Durham: Duke University Press

Mannathukkaren, N. (2001) Subalterns, Cricket and the 'Nation': The Silences of 'Lagaan' *Economic and Political Weekly* 8 December p4580-4588

Manuel, P. (1988) 'Popular Music in India 1901-1986' in *Popular Music* Vol.7 No.2 May pp. 157-176

Manuel, P. (1993) *Cassette Culture: Popular Music and Technology in North India* Chicago: University of Chicago Press

Mattelart, A. (1979) *Multinational Corporations and the Control of Culture* Brighton: Harvester

Mazid, A.. (1996) 'Sixty Years of Cinema from Arsam. Close Up of the Socio-political Image' in *Deep Focus* Vol.VI Nos.2 & 3 pp. 52-59

Meo, N. (2003) 'Bollywood exposes racism in Britain' in *The Times* 22.12.2003 p11

Mercer, K. (1994) *Welcome to the Jungle* London: Routledge

Mishra, V. (1985) 'Towards a Theoretical Critique of Indian Cinema' in *Screen* May-August Vol.26, Nos.3-4

Mishra, V. (2002) *Bollywood Cinema Temples of Desire* London: Routledge

Mishra, V. and Hodge, Bob (1991) What is (Post-) Colonialism? *Textual Practice* Volume 5 Number 3

Mishra, V., Jeffrey, P. and Shoesmith, B. (1989) 'The Actor as Parallel Text in Bombay Cinema' in *Quarterly Review of Film and Video* Vol.11, pp.49-67

Mital, A. (1995) *Cinema Industry in India – Pricing and Taxation* New Delhi: Indus Publishing Co

Mitra, A. (1994) 'An Indian Religious Soap Opera and the Hindu Image' in *Media, Culture and Society* Vol.16 pp. 149-155

Modood, T. *et al.* (1997) *Ethnic Minorities in Britain* London: Policy Studies Institute

Monda, A. (2002) Inreview with Mira Nair, in Spinelli, I. (ed.) *Indian Summer* Milano: Edizioni Olivares

Mukhopadhyay, D. (1995) *The Maverick Maestro – Mrinal Sen* New Delhi: Harper Collins

Mulvey, L (1975) 'Visual Pleasure and Narrative Cinema' in *Screen* Vol.16, No.3 (Autumn) pp.6-18

Mulvey, L. (1989) *Visual and Other Pleasures*, Bloomington: Indiana University Press

Naficy, H. (2003) *An Accented Cinema, Exilic and Diasporic Filmmaking* Princeton: Princeton University Press

Nagy, J. (2002) Film Review – Lagaan: Once Upon a time in India *Emergences* Volume 12 Number 2 p293-296

Nandy, A. (1981) 'The Popular Hindi Film Ideology and First Principles in India' *India International Centre* Quarterly Special Issue, Vol.8, No.1, March pp. 89-96

Nandy, A. (1987-88) 'An Intelligent Critic's Guide to Indian Cinema' Part I, II and III, December 1987, June 1988

Nandy, A. (1997) *The Secret Politics of Our Desires* Zed Books forthcoming

National Council for Applied Economic Research *Indian Market Demographics* New Delhi: NCAER

Negi, M. (1994-5) 'Mira Nair' in *Cinemaya* Autumn/Winter pp. 25-27

Nelmes, J. (Ed) (1996) *An introduction to Film Studies* London: Routledge

Newcomb, H. (1997) *Encyclopaedia of Television Volumes I, II and III*, Fitzroy: Dearborn

Niranjana, T. 'Integrating whose Nation? Tourists and Terrorists in Roja' in *Economic and Political Weekly* January 15, pp.79-82

Oomen, M. A. and Joseph, K. V. (1991) *Economics of Indian Cinema* New Delhi: Oxford and IBH Publishing Co

Oomen, T. K. (1990) *State and Society in India: Studies in Nation Building* New Delhi: Sage Publication

Page, D. and Crawley, W. (2001) *Satellites over South Asia* New Delhi: Sage

Paranjpye, S. (1988) 'Women in Cinema' in *Cinema in India* Vol.11 No.1 Jan-April pp. 15-19

Parekh, B. (2002) *Rethinking Multiculturalism* Cambridge, MA: Harvard University Press

Payne, M. (ed.) (1997) *A Dictionary of Cultural and Critical Theory* Oxford: Blackwell

Peach, C. (ed.) (1996) *Ethnicity in the 1991 Census* London: OPCS

Pendakur, M. (1989) 'New Cultural Technologies and the Fading Glitter of Indian Cinema' in *Quarterly Review of Film and Video*, Vol.11 pp. 69-78

Pendakur, M. (1995) 'Cinema of Resistance: – Recent Trends in Indian Documentary Film' Paper presented at the Yamagata International Documentary Film Festival, Tokyo, September pp.1-4

Pendakur, M. (1996) 'India's National Film Policy' in Moran, A. (Ed) *Film Policy* London: Routledge

Pendakur, M. and Subramanyam, R. (1996) 'Indian Cinema Beyond National Borders' in Sinclair, J. (Ed) *New Patterns in Global Television: Peripheral Vision* Oxford: Oxford University Press

Prasannarajan, S. (2002) Sex and Sensibility *India Today* Is Sex OK? August 2 p51

Price, S. (1994) *Media Studies* London: Pitman

Prasad, M. M. (1994) 'The State and Culture: Hindi Cinema on the Passive Revolution' Doctoral Dissertation submitted to the University of Pittsburgh

Raina, M. Z. (1986) ''I'm All Right Jack': Packaged Pleasures of the Middle Cinema' in *Journal of Popular Culture* Vol.20 Fall pp. 131-141

Rajadhyaksha, A. (2003) The Bollywoodization of Indian Cinema, Cultural Nationalism in a Global Arena *Inter-Asia Cultural Studies* Volume 4 Number 1

Rajadhyaksha, A. and Willemen, P. (1994) *Encyclopaedia of Indian Cinema* New Delhi: Oxford University Press

Rajadhyaksha, A. and Willemen, P. (eds.) (2nd edition, 1999) *Encyclopaedia of Indian Cinema* London: British Film Institute

Ramchandran, T. M. (ed) (1985) *70 Years of Indian Cinema (1913-1983)* Bombay: Cinema India-International

Rao, L. (1989) 'Woman in Indian Films – A Paradigm of Continuity and Change' in *Media, Culture and Society* Vol.11 pp. 443-458

Rao, M. (1988) 'Victims in Vigilante Clothing' in *Cinema in India* Oct.-Dec. pp.24-26

Rao, M. (1995) 'To be a Woman....' in VASUDEV, A. (Ed) *Frames of Mind* New Delhi: UBSPD

Ray, M. and Jacka, E. (1996) 'Indian Television: An Emerging Regional Force' in Sinclair, J. (Ed) *New Patterns in Global Television: Peripheral Vision* Oxford: Oxford University Press

Richards, A. (1995) *Hidden Pleasures: Negotiating the Myth of the Female Ideal in Popular Hindi Cinema* (Paper circulated at the SOAS Conference) 19-21 June

Said, E. (1978) *Orientalism* New York: Random House

Sarkar, B. (1995) 'Epic (Mis)takes: Nation, Religion and Gender on Television' in *Quarterly Review of Film and Video* Vol.16 No.1 pp. 59-75

Schiller, H. (1976) *Communication and Cultural Domination* White Plains, NY: Sharpe

Schlesinger, P. (1991) *Media, State and Nation: Political Violence and Collective Identities* London: Sage

Screen International (2001) Interview with UK Female Asian Director Gurinder Chadha about her new film *Bend it like Beckham* 28 September

Sen, A. (1993) 'Indian Pluralism' in *Monsoon* Vol.20, No.3, pp. 27-46

Shah, A. (1987) A Dweller in Two Lands: Mira Filmmaker, in *Cineaste* Volume 15 Number 3 p22-24

Sharma, S. D. (1994) 'India's precarious democracy: Between Crisis and resilience' review article in *Contemporary South Asia* Vol.3 No.2 pp.145-163

Sharma, S., Hutnyk, J. and Sharma, A. (eds.) (1996) *Dis-orienting rhythms: the Politics of the New Asian Dance Music* London: Zed Books

Shridar, K. T. (1989) 'An Elegy to Bombay' in *Deep Focus* Vol.2 No.1 September pp. 55-56

Shukla, S. (2003) *India Abroad* Princeton: Princeton University Press

Singh, S. (1989) 'The Epic (on) Tube: Plumbing the Depths of History' in *Cinema in India* Vol.3 No.2 pp. 77-101

Spivak, Gayatri C. (1987) *In Other Worlds: Essays in Cultural Politics* New York: Methuen

Spivak, Gayatri C. (1988) 'Can the Subaltern Speak?' in Nelson, C. and Grossberg L. (Eds) *Marxism and the Interpretation of Culture* Urbane: University of Illinois Press

Srinivas, L. (2002) The Active Audience: Spectatorship, social relations and the experience of cinema, in *India Media, Culture and Society* Volume 24 p155-173

Subramanyan, R. (1996) 'Class, Caste and Performance in 'Subaltern' Feminist Film Theory and Praxis: An Analysis of Rudaali' in *Cinema Journal* Vol.35, No.3 Spring pp. 34-57

Tasker, Y. (2002) *Fifty Contemporary Filmmakers* London: Routledge

Thomas, R. (1985) Indian Cinema: Pleasures and Populary in *Screen* Vol.26 No.3-4 pp. 116-131

Thomas, R. (1987) 'Mythologies and Modern India' in LUHR, W. (Ed) *World Cinema Since 1945* New York: Ungar

Thomas, R. (1989) 'Sanctity and Scandal – the Mythologisation of Mother India' in *Quarterly Review of Film and Video* Vol.11, No.3 Winter pp.11-30

Thomas, R. (1995) *Mother India Maligned: Film and Politics in Modern India – The Saga of Sanjay Dutt* (Paper circulated at the SOAS Conference) 19-21 June

The Times of India (2002) Films are our Gangotri, don't soil them Special Report 28 July

Tomlinson, J. (1991) *Cultural Imperialism: A Critical Introduction* Baltimore, MD: John Hopkins University

Tunstall, J. (1977) *The Media are American: Anglo-American Media in the World* London: Constable

Uberoi, P. (1995) *Imagining the Family: An Ethnography of Viewing 'Hum Aapke Hain Koun..!* Paper presented at the SOAS Conference on 'The Consumption of Popular Culture in India', 19-21 June

Unterberger, Amy L. (ed.) (1999) *The St James Women Filmmakers Encyclopaedia* Boston: Visible Ink Press

Valicha, K. (1988) *The Moving Image* Hyderabad: Orient Longman Limited

Varma, P.K. (1998) *The Great Indian Middle Class* New Delhi: Penguin

Varshney, A.. (1993) 'Contested Meanings: India's National Identity, Hindu Nationalism and the Politics of Anxiety' in *Daedalus* Vol.122, No.3, pp 227-261.

Vasudev, A. (1986) *The New Indian Cinema* Delhi: Macmillan.

Vasudev, A. (1995) *Frames of Mind Reflections on Indian Cinema* New Delhi: UBSPD.

Vasudevan, R. S. (1989) 'The Melodramatic Mode and the Commercial Hindi Cinema: Notes on Film History, Narrative and Performance in the 1950s' in *Screen* Vol.30 No.3.

Vasudevan, R. S. (1991) The Cultural Space of a Film Narrative: Interpreting Kismet (Bombay Talkies, 1943) in *The Indian Economic and Social History Review* Vol.28 No.2 pp. 171-185

Vasudevan, R. S. (1995a) 'Film Studies, New Cultural History and Experience of Modernity' in *Economic and Political Weekly* November 4 pp.2809-2814

Vasudevan, R. S. (1995b) *Bombay and its Public* (Paper circulated at the SOAS Conference) 19-21 June

Viegas, S. (1984) 'Lost in the Shadows' in *The Illustrated Weekly of India* February 12, pp. 40-45

Wadia, R. V. (1993) *Fearless: The Hunterwali Story* (75 minutes documentary).

Williams, P. and Chrisman, L. (eds.) (1994) *Colonial Discourse and Post-Colonial Theory: A Reader* London: Routledge and Kegan Paul

Williams, R. (1961) *The Long Revolution* London: Chatto and Windus

Young, Robert J.C. (2001) *Postcolonialism: An Historical Introduction* Oxford: Blackwell

Index

Films referred to in this book are in italics. For a full filmography of India see *Encyclopedia of Indian Cinema* (1994).

A
A Love Story (1942) 46
A Passage to India 70
Armaan 92
Aankhen 115
Achanak 121
Achut Kanya 5, 10, 27, 73, 74
Adi Shankaracharya 58, 131
Afghans 104
Akriet 137
Alaap 104
Alam Ara 15, 2
Amar, Akbar, Anthony 68
American cinema 9, 11, 53
Amritmanthan 16
Anaahat 138
Anand, Dev 102
Anand 101
Andaaz 28
Angulimal 60
Annadurai 65
Antarjali Yatra 75, 138
Apache Indian 105, 21
Aparajito 18, 32
Aparoop 130
Apna Group 121
Apu Trilogy 18
Apur Sansar 18, 32
Aravindan, G. 34, 62, 63, 134
Armaan 92, 112
Arnold, A. 102, 103, 111
Arnold and Hardiman 45
Arora, P. 53
Arth 91
Artistic 32, 34
Ashcroft *et al* 121
Asian film-makers 70, 72, 116-121
Assamese cinema 129-130
Australia 10
Awaara 5, 10, 18, 19, 29

Azmi, Kaifi 103
Azmi, Shabana 78, 89, 91

B
Bachchan, Amitabh 1, 29, 47, 48, 97, 110, 111, 112, 116
Badan Barphukan 130
Baghban 112
Baily, J. 104
Balagopalan, P 92
Banani 130
Bandit Queen 105
Banerji, S. 104
Bangladesh 10
Barnouw and Krishnaswamy 48, 101
Barsaat 28,102
Barua, P.C. 52
Battleship Potemkin 53
Beeman 48
Behind the Bush 81
Bell, Daniel 64
Bend it like Beckham 119
Benegal, Shyam 34, 44, 95
Binford 1, 13
Bengali 18, 24, 32, 129
Bengali Cinema 138
Bhagavad Gita The 42, 43, 57
Bhaji on the Beach 73, 119
Bhaktha Dhruva 130
Bhangra 104, 120, 121
Bharat Natyam 106
Bharatiya Janata Party (BJP) 110
Bharucha, R. 106
Bhatt, M. 91, 124
Bhattacharya, Basu 95
Bhattacharya, Rinki Roy 95, 101
Bhavai 21

Bhonsle, Asha 120
Bhoot 122
Bhuvan Shome 97
Bollywood 109, 141-142
Bombay 27, 99, 110, 113, 133
Bombay Dreams 4, 44
Bombay Films 3, 31, 45
Border 113
Bose, Amit 108
Bose, Devaki 52
Bose, Nitin 52
Brah 121
Braziel and Mannur 117
Bristi 130
Brown 40
Bruce, S. 41, 42
Buddha of Suburbia The 116
Buddhists 9, 40
Budgets of films 32, 51, 96, 97, 108
Burman, S.D. 103

C
Cabaret dancing 106
Calcutta 14, 18, 24, 32, 47, 53, 82, 86
Camera angles 23, 24, 34, 99, 116
Caribbean 10
Caste System 10, 11, 72-75
Chadha, Gurinder 71, 119, 143
Chakraborty 114
Chakravarty, S. 44, 47, 107
Chalte Chalte 112
Chandra, M. 106
Chandralekha 49, 132
Channi 61
Chaplin, Charlie 22
Charulatha 33
Chatterjee, Basu 95
Chatterjee, P 45

157

Chatterjee, S 115, 135
Chaudhvin Ka Chand 101
Chemmeen 134
Chetna 80
Chidambaram 62, 134
Child Marriage Restraint Act
    84
Children of the Desired Sex
    119
Chokher Bali 139
Chomanadudi 131
Chopra, Yash 2, 142
Chowringhee Lane 86, 138
CID 101
Clash of tradition 34
Classical Indian texts 11, 36, 77
Classical Indian theatre 20, 21
Classical Sanskrit 48, 91
Coconut Fair 13
Collective fantasies 46
Company 122
Congress Party 39, 65, 91
Cooper, Patience 14
Cuckoo 106

D
Dahavi, F 138
Daman 93
Damle, V. 52
Dance 12, 17, 21, 23, 29, 48,
    59, 81, 90, 99, 101,
    105, 107
Das Gupta 16, 52
Dasi 135
Dastak 82
de Sica, Vittorio 32
Deewana 81
Deewar 29, 44
Dehlavi, Jamil 70
Deo, Shashi 106
Derné and Jadwin 123, 124
Devdas 115
Devgan, Ajay 114
Devi 18, 33, 60
Devotional films 25
Dharap, B.V. 50
Dharma 41, 42, 43, 46, 56, 57,
    61
Dharmaraj, Rabindra 92
Dharmat 56
Dharmendra 48
Dhawan, D 116
Dhillon-Kashyap 70
Dil Chahta Hai 115
Dhondy, F 10
Dil to pagal hai 110, 112

Dilwale Dulhania Le Jayenge
    3, 4, 110, 111, 112, 115
Dil Se 2, 3
Dissanayake, W. 29
Dissanayake and Sahai 31, 48,
    61, 124
Distinctiveness of Indian
    cinema 13, Ch.2
Distribution system 20
Divine intervention 43
Dixit, Madhuri 46, 47, 113
Do Anjane 78
Do Bigha Zamin 101
Don Juan 14
Doordarshan 3, 110
Dream sequences/wet saris 81
Dubey 109
Duniya Na Mane 16, 78
Dudrah 120, 121
Dutt, Guru 12, 17, 95
Dutt, Sanjay 47
Dweepa 132
Dwyer 110

E
Earth 117
East and South Africa 10
Economics of film production
    20, 39, 49, 51, 121-122
Ek Ristha 112
Elippathayam 134
Elphinstone Bioscope Company
    14
Emancipation of women Ch.5
Emergency in 1975 48
Esthappan 134
Ethnicity 66, 69, 70
Europe 10

F
Face to Face 34
Family melodramas 27
Fearless, The Hunterwali Story
    17
Filhaal 94, 94
Film Finance Corporation
    (FFC) 50
Film Censorship 52, 53, 124,
    126
Filmmaker 119
Financial entrepreneurs 52
Filhaal 93
Fire 117
Fiza 112
Folk theatre 19, 21, 95

G
Gabbar Singh 31
Gadar 111, 113, 114
Gandhi 27, 40
Gandhi Mrs 48
Ganesha 42
Gangaajal 114
Gangster films 12
Garam Hava 66, 67
Gardish 98
Garga, B.D. 6, 48, 52, 65, 67,
    90, 130, 131, 132, 134,
    137, 138
Geetha, J. 44
Genres 12, 25, 26, 27
Ghatak, Ritwik 12, 18, 25, 34,
    95, 96, 97, 138
Ghata Shradhdha 131, 132
Ghazal 103
Ghose, Gautam 34
Ghosh, Parvati 83
Gilroy 116
Godzilla 143
Gokulsing 109, 110, 115
Golden Age of Indian popular
    cinema 17
Gopalakrishnan, Adoor 18, 25,
    34, 95, 124, 133, 134,
    135, 141
Gope 70
Gopinath, G. 105, 117
Goswamy 97
Govinda 116
Granth Sahib 61
Griffin 143
Guide 102
Gulel 93
Gulzar, M 93
Gulzar et al 5

H
Halodhia Choraya Baodhan
    Khai 130
Hansa Geethe 132
Hardgrave, Jr R.L. 65
Hayward 118
Heat and Dust 70, 116
Helen 106
Hero No.1 115
Hindu Widow's Remarriage
    Act. 84
Hindus/Hinduism 9, 27, 40, 41-
    42, 66, 68
Hindustan Ki Kasam 111
Hindutva 110
Historical development 13

Hkhagaroloi Boho Door 130
Hollywood 14, 15, 18, 19, 22,
   23, 98
Hollywood cinema 22
Hollywood musicals 18, 22, 23,
   98
Home and the World 31
Horror films 12
*Hum Aapke Hain Koun
   (HAKH)* 3, 110, 111, 115
Hussain, Waris 70

I
I... Proud to be an Indian 119,
   120
Ideology 19-20
Impact of Hollywood 22, 98-99
Import of foreign films 50, 122,
   143
Indian Family 13, 44, 110
India Today 124
India's secularism 40-41, 64
Indrasabha 49
Irani, H 22
Ishanou 60
Islam 56, 64
Ivan the Terrible 53
Iyer, G. V. 58

J
Jagdeep 101
Jagirdar 16
Jai Santoshi Ma 59, 60
Jain, R.D. 50
Jains 9, 40
Jait Re Jait 137
Jalsaghar 18, 32
Jayalalitha 65
Jeevana Nataka 16
Jewel in the Crown 70
Jhanak Jhanak Payal Baaje 106
Jodi No.1 116
Johar, K 142
Joshi 141
Juge Juge Sangram 130
Jurassic Park 24, 52, 143

K
Kaagaz Ke Phool 16
Kabir, M. 49, 51, 102
Kabir and Snell 102, 103
Kaddu 131
Kaho naa Pyaar Hai 111
Kajol 113
Kakar, S. 46
Kala Bazar 102

Kalpana 106
Kalyug 44
Kama Sutra 118
Kannada Cinema 47, 130-132
Kannathil Muthamittal 133
Kapadia, Dimple 90
Kapoor, Karisma 113
Kapoor, Kareena 113
Kapoor, Raj 10, 12, 17, 22
Kapoor, Rishi 81
Kapoor, Shashi 29
Karan Arjun 112
Karanth, Prema 83, 85
Karma 42, 56
Karnad, Girish 131, 132
Kartavya 26
Karun, Shaji 18, 34, 134
Kasaravalli, Girish 59, 132
Kashmir issue 70
Katz and Wedell 143
Kaul, Mani 34, 95, 119
Kauravas 43
Keechaka Vadham 6
Kerala 58, 62, 133, 134
Khabi khushi Kabbie Gham 110
Khalnayak 98
Khan, Amir 112
Khan, Mehboob 16, 17, 95
Khan, Nusrat Fateh Ali 105
Khan, Salman 112
Khan Sharukh 47, 93, 112, 115
Khanna, Rajesh 48
Khanna, S.P. 67
Kismet 29
Kissing 80
Kohli, A. 39
Kohraam 111
Koi Mil Gaya 111, 112
Kotikobba 132
Krishna Lila 21
Krishnamurthy, Kavita 49
Kuch Kuch Hota Hai 3, 110,
   112, 115
Kumar, Dilip 115
Kumar, Gulshan 52
Kumar, Kishore 49
Kummaty 134
Kunwara 116
Kureishi, Hanif 71, 116
Kyon 92, 115

L
Lachit Barphukan 130
Lagaan 2, 113, 114
Lajmi, Kalpana 83, 92
Lakshya 115

Lal Badshah 111
Lanka Dahan 57
Laurel and Hardy 22
Lee 143
Leitch 144
Levich, J. 96
LOC Kargil 115
London Kills Me 115
Long 116
Lord Krishna 43
Lumière brothers 13

M
Macey 121
Macnab 118
Madan, J.F. 14
Madan Theatre 14
Madan, T.N. 55, 56
Madhumati 95, 101
Madras 65
Mahabharata, The 15, 19, 20,
   28, 42, 43, 55, 57,
   98, 110
Mahanagar 32, 82
Mahaprithivi 97
Mahmood Talat 120
Main Hoon Na 93
Maitra, P. 51
Major Saab 111
Majumdar, D. 49, 50
Majumdar, B. 113
Malayalam 24, 32, 47, 50, 126,
   129, 132-135
Malaysia 10
Mangeskhar, Lata 103
Maniram Dewan 130
Mankekar 110
Manmohan 16
Mannathukkaren 114
Manuel, P. 103, 120
Manusmriti 43, 77
Manzil 16
Marathi Cinema 136-138
Marx brothers 22
Masala 45
Masoom 91
Mattelart 143
Mauritius 10
Maya 56
Mazid, A. 129, 130
Meghe Dhaka Tara 96
Mehta, K. 24, 34
Meo 120
Mercer 121
Merchant, Ismail 70, 116
Metha, D. 117

Metha, V. 69, 137
Middle Cinema 91
Mitr My Friend 93
Mirpus 104
Mishra, V. 3, 20
Mishra and Hodge 121
Mission Kashmir 111, 112
Mississippi Masala 71,118, 120
Mital 50
Modern Music Television
 (MTV) 23-24, 98
Modood *et al* 116
Mohabbatein 111
Mohini Bhasmasur 105
Monda 143
Monsoon Wedding 118, 119,
 124, 143
Mother India 19, 29, 44, 79
Movie Moguls, The 52
Mr and Mrs Iyer 93
Mr. and Mrs. 55 101
Mrityudaata 111
Mukesh 103, 120
Mukhamukham 134
Mukhopadhyay, D. 97
Mulvey, L. 82, 123
Mumtaz Ali 106
Music 15, 23, 101-103
Music among British Asians
 103-105, 120-121
Music Room 18, 32
Muthu 133
My Beautiful Laundrette 71,
 116

N
Naa Tum Jaano Naa Hum 112
Naanak Nam Jahaz Hai 61
Nadia 17
Naficy 142
Nagy 114
Nair, Mira 71, 117, 118, 119,
 124, 143
Nandy, A. 47
Narayan, Udit 49
Nargis 44
Narrative structure 19
National Council for Economic
 research 109
National Film Development
 Corporation 50
Natya and Sangeet 49
Naushad 103
Nautanki 21
Nautch 49
Nehru 27, 40
Nepal 10

Nigam Sonu 120
Nihalani, Govind 34
Niranjana, T. 41
Nirmala, V. 83
Nizhalkkuthu 135
North America 10
Nurjehan 102

O
Oomen, T.K. 47
Oomen and Joseph 50
Oor Iravu 133
Our Indian Empire 13

P
Padwal, A. 120
Page and Crawley 109, 110
Pakeeza 107
Palekar 137, 138
Panam 133
Pandavas 43
Papoori 130
Parama 88, 89
Paranjpye, Sai 83, 91
Parasakthi 133
Parekh 116
Parsees 9, 21, 40, 68-69
Parsi theatre 19, 21, 98
Patalghar 139
Pather Panchali 18, 32
Patel, Jabbar 137
Patil, Smita 92
Patwardhan, Nachiket and
 Jayoo 137
Payne 4
Pendakur, M. 12
Pestonjee 69
Phalke, D.G. 12, 14, 15, 17, 55,
 105, 136
Phaniyamma 84, 86, 131
Piravi 134
Pokkuveyil 134
Prasad, M.M. 80, 81
Prasannarajan 127
Pratidhwani 130
Prince Arjuna 42
Prohor 139
Pundalik 14
Pyaasa 18, 101

Q
Qawwali 105
Quarterly Review of Film and
 Video 1

R
Raakhee 90
Rafi 120
Rahman, A.R. 4, 144
Rai, Himansu 15, 52
Raina, M.Z. 90, 91, 92
Raja Harischandra 2, 14, 15,
 44, 55, 105
Rajadhyaksha and Willemen 5,
 10, 16, 75, 92
Rajnigandha 137
Raktha Kaneeru 132
Ram Lakhan 44
Ram Lila 21
Rama 43, 55, 65
Rama Rao, (NTR) N.T. 65
Ramayana The 15, 19, 20, 26,
 42, 43, 55, 57, 77, 98, 110
Ramchandran, (MGR) M.G. 65,
 132, 133
Rao, N.T. Rama 135
Rao, Narasinga 135
Ramachandran T.M. 105
Rao Saheb 85, 86
Rat Trap 34
Rathnam, Mani 27, 40, 41, 62,
 68, 99, 133
Ray, Satyajit 18, 25, 32, 60, 75,
 82, 86, 138, 141
Refugee 110
Rekha 101
Relationship between Hindus
 and Muslims 11,
 40, 41, 66, 67, 68, 113
Revathi 93
Richards, A. 79, 80, 81
Ritual, The 59
Roja 40, 41, 110, 133
Roshan, H. 111, 112
Roy, Bimal 17, 73, 95, 101
Rudaali 90
*Rules: Pyar ka Superhit
 Formula* 92

S
Sadgati 75
Saeed Akhtar Mirza 67
Safri Boyz 121
Sagoo 121
Sahani, K. 95
Sahib Bibi Aur Ghulam 101
Saigal, K.L. 103, 115
Salaam Bombay 118
Salamalo 27, 58
Salim Langde Pe Mat Ro 67
Sammy and Rosie Get Laid 71
Samna 137

Samskara 60, 74, 131, 132
Sanatana Dharma 56
Sandhyaraag 130
Sankalpat 130
Sankar, Uday 106
Sanskrit drama 21, 98
Sanskrit theatre 20, 98
Sant Sakhu 58
Sant Tukaram 24, 26, 58
Sant Tulsidas 58
Sarfarosh 110
Sardar 110
Satellite Channels 110, 115
Sathyu, M.S. 66, 67
Sati 79
Sati Anjani 79
Sati Ansuya 79
Sati Parvati 79
Sati Savitri 79
Sati Seeta 79
Sati Sulochana 130
Satya 3, 122
Satyam Shivam Sundaram 59
Savarkar 40
Schiller 143
Schlesinger 143
Screen International 119
Secularisation 64
Sen, Amartya 9
Sen, Aparna 34, 83, 93
Sen, Mrinal 25, 34
Sex scenes 124, 126, 127, 144
Shah, Chandulal 52
Shah, Naseeruddin 91
Shah, A. 118
Shahani, Kumar 18, 34, 44
Shantaram, V. 12, 15, 16, 17, 24, 52
Shanu, Kumar 49
Sharma, S.D. 60
Sharma et al 121
Sholay 29, 45, 48, 61, 114, 124
Shukla 119, 121
Sight and Sound 32
Sign of the Cross 14
Sikhs 9, 40, 60, 61
Singapore 10
Singing in the Rain 23
Sira 119, 20
Sircar, B.N. 52
Sita 26, 43, 57, 77
Smriti Chitre 85, 137
Song and dance sequences 23, 81, 101
Sparsh 91
Speed 143
Spivak 121

Sree 420 18,101
Sri Lanka 10
Srinivas, L. 123
Subarnarekha 96
Sujata 11, 73, 74
Suraiya 102
Surendra 102
Suryvansham 111

T
Taal 2
Tabarana Kathe 132
Taboot Procession 14
Tagore, Rabindranath 33
Tamasha 21
Tamil Cinema 24, 31, 47, 65, 132-133
Tamil Nadu 21, 65, 98
Tarang 44
Tasker 117
Telugu Cinema 31, 47, 65, 132, 135, 136
Terukkuttu 98
Thampu 134
Thanawala, F.B. 14
Thangaratnam 133
The Great Train Robbery 14
The Long Revolution 4
The Magnificent Seven 30
The Wild Bunch 30
The Wrestlers 14
Thodasa Rumani Ho Jaye 137
Thodisi Bewafayi 78
Thomas, Rosie 12, 29, 31, 79
Times of India 13
Titanic 143
Tomlinson 143
Torney, R.G. 14
Tribal Dress 81
True Lies 143
Tunstall 143

U
Uberoi, P. 45, 46
Umbartha 137
Umrao Jan 107
Uncle Tom's Cabin 14
Unterberger 117
Urvashi, S 92
Uski Kahani 95

V
Valicha, K. 70
Vamsa Vriksha 132
Varma, Ram Gopal 122, 124
Varma 109
Varshney, A. 39, 40, 41
Vaskrupurush 138
Vasthuhara 134
Vasudev, A. 14, 16
Vasudevan, R. 39
Velakkari 133
Violence and gory deaths 48
Virdi 93
Vithinatakam 21
Voyeurism 82
Vulgarity 46
Vyjayanthimala 106

W
Wadia, R.V. 17
Walker, Johnny 70, 101
Water 117
Whirling the Worlds 14
Williams, Raymond 4, 10
Williams and Chrisman 121

Y
Yadein 112
Yagnik, Alka 120
Yakshagana 21
Yatra of Bengal 21
Young 121

Z
Zakhm 114
Zanjeer 19